QUALITY CIRCLE MANAGEMENT

quality circle management

THE

HUMAN

SIDE

OF

QUALITY

Harry Katzan, Jr.

TAB Professional and Reference Books

Division of TAB BOOKS Inc.

Blue Ridge Summit, PA

A Petrocelli book
FIRST EDITION
FIRST PRINTING

Library of Congress Cataloging in Publication Data

Katzan, Harry.
    Quality circle management.

    Bibliography: p.
    Includes index.
    1. Quality circles. I. Title.
HD66.K38 1989   658.4'036   87-36047
ISBN 0-8306-3386-3

CONTENTS

FOREWORD

In today's fast-paced world, nearly everyone wants to obtain more output with the same input. Some claim it can be achieved with *excellence*, others with *productivity*, and still others with *quality*. The truth is obvious. Excellence plus productivity do, in fact, equal quality. Quality is about people, commitment, passion, and pride. One way of achieving it is through participative management—the practice of letting people do a good job.

Unequivocally, quality is simultaneously a profession, an attitude, and a means of viewing the true goals of an enterprise. It is totally naive, on the other hand, to expect every manager and every coworker to be exactly on the beam. Only through participation and cooperation can the multifaceted ideas of a team be merged into a coherent whole. One means of achieving quality is by making people part of the solution and not a part of the problem. We recommend *quality circles*. In this book, the concept is placed in the context of automation, decision-making, and the human side of enterprise.

The famous American author John Gardner is often quoted for recognizing that, "Democracy is measured not by its leaders doing extraordinary things, but by its citizens doing extraordinarily well."

O. R. Petrocelli
Editor-in-Chief

PREFACE

There was a time when Japanese scientists, engineers and businessmen flocked to the United States to observe business operations and new product ideas. In recent years, however, the trend has been reversed, such that Americans and Europeans now go to Japan to learn. This is reminiscent of an old story.

A primitive tribe captured an American, a Frenchman and a Japanese. Each was given a final request prior to being executed. The Frenchman asked to hear the French national anthem just one more time. The Japanese requested that he be allowed to give his quality control lecture just one more time. Whereupon, the American asked to be executed first so he would not have to listen to yet another Japanese lecture on quality control.

This book is not just another lecture on quality control; it concerns a participative management technique that really works: quality circles.

A *quality circle* is a small group of workers who meet regularly on a voluntary basis to analyze problems and recommend solutions to management. The organizational sphere of activity of quality circle participants is the area in which they work. The concept of a quality circle originated in Japan to assist in solving quality problems in manufacturing, and has since been applied to a variety of related managerial problems throughout the world in diverse disciplines. It has been said that Americans are motivated to making the unknown known, whereas the Japanese are motivated to making the known work and function better. As a management discipline, therefore, quality circle methods are strictly pragmatic and clearly fall into the latter category.

The primary application of quality circles has been in the area of quality achievement; however, the concepts are as applicable to banking and other forms of commerce as they are to manufacturing.

The basic philosophy underlying quality circles is that quality awareness through participative management can not only identify the problem situations but can also assist management in solving them. As a Theory Y discipline, the quality circle concept recognizes that people know their jobs best and want to contribute to the success of their company, if given the chance to do so.

A quality circle is a form of group dynamics in which each member's participation has a synergistic effect on the other members' work behavior in identifying and solving problems. This book shows how a quality circle operates and how to put it to work for your organization. Three main topics are covered:

- Quality circle principles
- Quality circle methods
- Strategic planning for quality circles

Within these topics, the innate value of voluntary small-group participation is explained and the policies, procedures and applicable methods are described. Organizational implications as well as implementation considerations are covered in detail. Finally, success elements are identified and the dynamics of quality circle activities are introduced.

Since we participate in a high-tech environment and many problems of productivity and quality are associated with the increased use of automation, it would be remiss not to place the subject matter in its proper context. Accordingly, the core material is supplemented with chapters on the concerns of automation, human relations, and decision-making.

This book is written for executives, managers, administrators, planners and analysts. The subject of quality circles is as applicable to banking and data processing as it is to manufacturing and the service industries. No particular background is needed to readily comprehend the topics covered, but an appreciation of management problems and experience in solving them would serve as useful prerequisites.

It is a pleasure to acknowledge my wife, Margaret, who assisted with the manuscript preparation and was a good partner during the project.

Harry Katzan, Jr.
Fribourg, Switzerland

Part One:

AUTOMATION

I

CONCERNS OF AUTOMATION

Introduction

Without question, we are active participants in a high-tech society wherein many problems of productivity and quality are associated with automation. To assert that the problems *are* caused by automation is too strong a statement.

There is an old adage that says you should sweep your own doorstep first. So, management should take a close look at its relationship to the entire process of automation. Clearly, the concept of economic man and the techniques of deductive reasoning so strongly espoused by business schools must be supplemented by inductive reasoning and philosophical thinking. Managers must manage automation, not control it. Managers must also ensure that systems of automation are designed so that they can evolve into dynamic facilities that can change with the enterprise. In the future, there will be no throwaway system because costs and complexity will prevent it.

As we enter a knowledge-based era, wherein

information is a key resource, our personal models of the enterprise must incorporate appropriate conditions and indicators to profitably use this information. We are highly dependent on automation technology, and mankind has to adapt to this dependence. Moreover, systems knowledge is distributed and interfaces are imposed by outside constraints; this complicates the situation.

In short, distributed knowledge is precisely what employees have, and productivity is achieved through their participation.

Societal Responsibility, Social Bottlenecks

Automation, including computers as a discipline, has progressively been a central theme in all areas of social activity, including:

Economics
Industry and commerce
Art and science
Administration and government
International relations
Education
Culture and daily life

The key question is, "What forms of automation will be required to meet future needs generated by environmental changes and to avoid societal bottlenecks resulting from short-term goals and traditional organizational dynamics?"

Managers are accustomed to dealing with "macro" systems demanded by the above problem domain. However, unless a manager possesses the proper organizational perspective, he or she can be unprepared to handle long-range problems concerning the societal impact of automation.

As stated above, we are highly dependent upon automation technology in today's complex business world. By this, we mean instrumentation, equipment (various kinds of hardware), and software and the organization to support it. A subject not often discussed at management levels is, "What can be done if automation fails?" Most large corporations, including banks and the Federal Government, would fail immediately if automation were to fail.

Underlying this total dependence on automation is the universal attitude that the situation is something with which mankind must be prepared to live. Must this necessarily be the case? The present situation, at least as we view it, is that systems knowledge is distributed throughout the organization. For the marginal rewards of compatibility and transportability, we are attempting to control the systems on which we depend by surrendering to public standards groups and de facto vendor conventions instead of fully utilizing the knowledge inherent in the organization.

The Future Role of Automation

It is useful to place automation, as a concept, in a world view from which we can put some perspective on our own activities. The future role of automation can be placed into four categories, the first of which is *to increase productivity in low-productivity areas*:

- Product quality and productivity in secondary industries, such as banking and manufacturing, have been greatly improved through the use of computers, advanced manufacturing processes, control systems and advanced technology.
- Productivity in primary industries, such as agriculture and fishing, has remained unchanged.
- Productivity in tertiary industries, such as distribution and service, has improved only slightly.

The result has been a noticeable social imbalance which, through ordinary feedback cycles, has begun to adversely affect the progress already made.

The second category is *to enhance international cooperation and permit advantageous international competition*. In the modern world, no nation—or even commercial business—can be self-sufficient. It is necessary to cultivate information as a new resource, comparable in a logical sense to food, energy and people. Users and processors of information must be made aware of the need for intercommunication.

The third category is *to save energy and other valuable resources*. One of the key problems for our generation is to find out how to use the world's resources effectively and to preserve many of the natural resources that we now have.

The final category is *to plan effectively for an aged society*. It is no secret that our society is aging at an increasing rate; concomitantly, there have been rapid increases in medical costs and welfare expenses. Force is exerted on the problem of aging by inflationary trends, but this is definitely not the complete picture. There is also a technical component to aging—advanced diagnostic tools, new medicines, and dramatic new developments including transplants and artificial organs.

Productivity

Productivity is in the news these days as an effective means of counteracting the downward effects of various economic forces. The goal of most industries has been to strive for total productivity through specialization and economy of scale. Clearly, these advantages are inherent in traditional assembly, fabrication, and molding processes in manufacturing; moreover, the same advantages are currently being espoused by proponents of modern information systems which incorporate data bases, office automation and decision support systems, in addition to the often-used and much-maligned concept of management information systems. Ironically, conventional data processing and online systems are now regarded as "old stuff," together with factory automation and flexible manufacturing systems.

A key point, of course, is that total productivity has meaning only if analyzed from the standpoint of the enterprise as a whole. Another important consideration that embodies job satisfaction is that the contribution of individuals, although important, is no more than a part of productivity; in fact, emphasis on job satisfaction tends to mask the real issues. The final point concerns the notion that productivity is simply the replacement of workers with machines.

Automation—and most of us are convinced that it is a very good concept—requires a balanced approach that necessitates a close look at the entire system.

BEFORE INDUSTRIALIZATION

The notion of productivity is rooted in history, but not as far back as most people think. Before industrialization, there was little need to even consider the subject of productivity. Without proper commerce or storage facilities, the incentive for a farmer to produce more than the immediate family could consume was practically nonexistent. Through bartering, some excess crops could be traded for other goods. Otherwise, there was no need for a higher level of production than could be comfortably achieved. Actually, this mode of behavior is a direct carryover from feudal periods, when additional crops were taken directly by an overseer, often a king or ruling party.

AFTER MECHANIZATION

With the introduction of farm implements, mechanization was largely based on personal convenience rather than increased production. In subsequent cultures, starting with ancient Greece and the Roman Empire and extending through periods of slavery and early industrialization (i.e., the early "sweatshops"), increased production from the viewpoint of the individual served only as a means of avoiding punishment in a variety of forms.

WITH MONEY

With the advent of money as a medium of exchange, together with a sufficient level of industrialization, the output of the production process became of prime importance. The level of input was largely ignored as long as output continued to increase. This naturally led to divisions of labor and to specialization aided by various machines. Rudimentary considerations of productivity effectively started during this period.

SPECIALIZATION

In many ways, productivity is associated with the division of labor and specialization. In the professions, these concepts are desirable. In fact, it is precisely these elements that make a direct contribution to productivity—at least initially—because they pave the way for:

- A higher level of individual worker skill(s)
- Increased work-flow organization
- The use of machines to augment the worker

Productivity elements such as these have enhanced the competitiveness of the work environment. At first, the guise was patriotic duty: enabling one's country to compete effectively in the international marketplace. Thus, workers were encouraged to be more productive because it provided a means for the country to price its products below the prices of competing countries. Lately, however, the guise for increased productivity has been more desperate: survival. Many business enterprises find it increasingly difficult to compete because their competitors have become *more* than productive people; they have more productive systems, which is essentially a means of "working smarter."

PRODUCTIVE SYSTEM

A productive system contains five basic ingredients:

- Necessary resources
- Optimum proportion of resources
- Maximum utilization of each resource
- A productive environment
- Proper interaction among resources

With these elements combined effectively, an operating structure is achieved that is appropriate for attaining the "success factors" of the organization. These factors can be units, rejects, or other countable measures of productivity. The production process combines elements of the five ingredients in optimum proportions, permitting each to be best utilized while fully interacting properly in a productive environment. Thus, people are utilized where human skills yield the greatest payoff, and machines are likewise utilized where the payoff is also the largest. As suggested in Figure 1.1, the process exists in an environment containing factors for training, organization, leadership and quality.

A boundary separates the internal parts of the productive system from its environment, and there should be a constant pressure to expand the boundary so that it is incorporated more fully into the total operational environment. A familiar example of this expansion is the accepted concept that quality emanates from the top through training and other management programs.

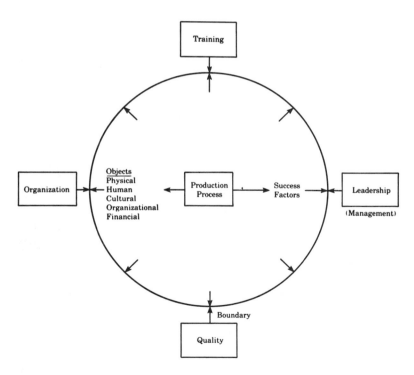

FIGURE 1.1   A PRODUCTIVE SYSTEM.

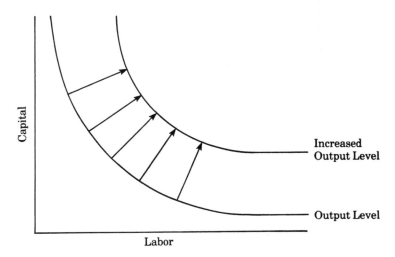

FIGURE 1.2 FIGURATIVE INCREASE IN PRODUCTION (DEPICTED AS A PRODUCTION FUNCTION ACHIEVED THROUGH A PRODUCTIVITY INCREASE).

An increase in productivity achieved by combining the factors of production in an advantageous manner is essentially the same as a shift in the production function, as suggested by Figure 1.2. This is the old "guns and butter" diagram that denotes the amount of each that can be purchased with a given amount of money. In such cases, the dislocation of the production function is normally associated with several major benefits:

- An increase in the standard of living
- Price stabilization
- Increased competitiveness
- Improved profitability

The end result, of course, is simply the fact that increased productivity leads to increased chances for survival. In a competitive market system, a progressive company employing new technology can operate offensively with a healthy increase in employment. Companies not employing new technology must operate defensively, and employment can correspondingly be problematic. Thus, a defensive attitude of individuals towards various forms of automation may in fact be unfounded and may end up as a self-defeating strategy. In the long run, companies with high productivity are associated with high profit increases and growth in employment.

ORGANIZATIONAL STRATEGY

An enterprise can approach the subject of productivity either offensively or defensively. The offensive team is deployed when it is necessary to increase profit margins or the market share. The defensive team comes in when competitors have introduced new technology and it is necessary to guard one's position. The end result may be the same; however, the best defense may be a strong offense.

Profitability is directly related to productivity, and the reasons are straightforward:

- When the cost of labor and materials is the same among competitors, the company with the highest productivity can have the highest profit margins.
- Companies with the highest productivity tend to control the larger share of the market.

At the same time, it is important to recognize that productivity does not necessarily relate directly to cost reduction, but it does in fact imply the optimum use of available resources.

Heretofore, productivity has been regarded as a labor problem or as a case of increased automation. It is only recently that informed management circles have involved the total organization in productivity and have recognized the significance of relationships among organizational units. Several key elements have been identified:

- *Top-management involvement* is needed in an effective productivity improvement program.
- *Worker involvement* is needed to identify areas where improvement can be made and for possible courses of action problem resolution.
- Quantitative aspects of *productivity improvement* through isolation and resolution should be enhanced by measurement and analysis.
- *Open communication* between management and workers should be encouraged, especially with regard to quality effectiveness procedures.
- *Productivity objectives* should be established and evaluated on a periodic basis.
- The total productivity program should be reviewed by disinterested parties to insure objectivity.

Many organizations have utilized the concept of a steering committee to govern the actions of mana-

gerial personnel and to ensure that needed resources are available. Effective productivity programs require strategic planning involvement
and an increased level of employee participation.

Big Can Be Beautiful

It may have seemed an element of fate when, in
1975, the late economist E.F. Schumacher selected the title *Small is Beautiful* for his noted
book on small-scale economics. Publication of the
book coincided with the microelectronics boom
and became somewhat of a handbook for certain
segments of that enterprise. Schumacher stressed
three points with regard to the needs for methods
and equipment:

1. They must be inexpensive enough to make
   them individually accessible.
2. They must be designed for small-scale applications.
3. They must be compatible with our need for
   creativity.

It is unfortunately the case that many persons
have taken "small is beautiful" as a mandate to
sidestep the real issues in automation in favor of
"island" solutions to problems requiring systems
integration within their organizations. However,
most substantial forms of automation started out
as small systems, and small systems are not a
priori more efficient than larger ones. In short,
"big, too, can be beautiful. . ."

It is important to stress at this time that the

primary interest of productivity and automation is growth. It is necessary to maintain all of the positive things with a small business and to translate them directly to a large operation.

Elements of Automation

It is evident that systems should be engineered so that they can benefit from advances in technology. Automation is no more a collection of computational tools than a set of implements constitutes a manufacturing process. *Automation* is an entourage of facilities working in harmony by passing tasks from one resource to the next.

Our concerns for automation are fivefold:

- *Functionability*—have we applied the latest technology?
- *Operability*—has the system been designed so we can manage it?
- *Integrity*—does the system provide consistent and correct results?
- *Productivity*—does the system provide an avenue for growth or is it simply a reallocation of resources?
- *Completeness*—does the system provide a total solution?

Given this set of concerns, the solution space is three-dimensional. A system—in fact, *any* system—must exhibit congruence, auditability, and controllability. *Congruence* ensures that the most appropriate systems design concept is applied at the proper time. *Auditability* ensures that the system can be demonstrated to perform its intended function. *Controllability* is concerned with whether operation of the system is effectively controlled by management.

In the area of congruence, a good system design causes the operation to become less tractable as people are replaced by systems. On the other hand, as internal organizational processes become simplified, people are freed for more creative work.

In the area of auditability, two common measures are *predictability* and *visibility*. The operation of a system should be demonstrably predictable, and deviations from established patterns should be readily observable by management.

Two tests of controllability are granularity and specificity. The simple test of *granularity* is whether a subsystem is designed so that its operation constitutes an acceptable risk to management. A test of *specificity* is whether the result of passing an informational resource from one subsystem to another is predictable.

The New Paradigm for Automation

It is time that managers of automation developed a new mental model (i. e., a new paradigm) of the processes they control. This need is mandated by the shift from a manufacturing process-oriented approach to a knowledge-based society with associated goods and services. The long-accepted assumption that quantitative increases in the production of goods and services as evidence of human progress no longer commands general agreement.

Technology must be linked to articulated purposes, and the new paradigm must reflect the true situation and not a social conception of it. There is an old British adage, "Experts on tap, not on top." Managers must be domain experts who can comprehend the technology they manage and can effectively look into the future.

The *rational manager* of tomorrow must comprehend and employ the following paradigms:

- *Feedback*—in control theory, the intelligent regulator is external to the regulated system
- *Pullback*—in knowledge-based systems, the regulated system is intelligent and the intelligent regulator is internal to it

An intelligent system is free because it has the ability to act according to internalized goals.

Clearly, the success of participative management lies in the pullback paradigm.

Part Two:

QUALITY CIRCLES

II

QUALITY CIRCLE PRINCIPLES

Introduction

A quality circle is a small group of workers who meet regularly on a voluntary basis to analyze problems and recommend solutions to management. The organizational sphere of activity of quality circle participants is the area in which they work. This concept originated in Japan to assist in solving quality problems in manufacturing and has since been applied to a variety of related managerial problems throughout the world in diverse disciplines. In fact, quality circles were originally known as "quality control (QC) circles" in Japan and are still sometimes called QC circles there. Quality circles have been used in both private and public enterprises in countless variations. To a greater or lesser degree most organizations that adopt the quality circle concept have adapted it to their particular needs.

Clearly, the primary application domain of quality circles is that of quality achievement; however, quality achievement can take a variety of forms ranging from worker behavior to management cooperation. Moreover, quality achievement may or may not involve high technology, and is as applicable to banking as it is to manufacturing.

The basic philosophy underlying quality circles is that quality awareness through participative management can not only identify problem situations but can also assist management in solving them. Clearly, workers know their jobs best and want to contribute to the success of their company if given the opportunity to do so. With regard to Theory X and Theory Y management styles, which are well-known, the use of quality circles is a Theory Y approach. A quality circle is a form of group dynamics; members collaborate to identify and solve problems, and the group members have a synergistic effect on one another's work behavior and on their individual contributions to collaborative quality circle activities.

Most descriptions of quality circles begin with a heavy dose of history with the commendable objective of attempting to describe the salient benefits of quality circle activities and to preserve the origins of the techniques. While there is certainly some benefit in history, it is also important to recognize that cultural differences imply that an approach that works in one country may not be directly transferable to another country, thus lessening the overall benefit of a historical perspective. As an alternative and perhaps a more direct approach to quality circle dynamics, the following list of attributes is presented:

- Participation in quality circle activities is voluntary.
- A quality circle is a small group composed of four to six people in small shops, six to ten people in medium-sized shops, and perhaps eight to twelve people in large-sized shops.
- Quality circle members do similar work, or their work is related in a logical sense so that members normally work as part of a team to achieve a common goal.
- Quality circles meet regularly to discuss and solve problems that they identify or that are proposed to their circle leader.
- Every circle has a formal leader responsible for the operation of the circle. The leader is usually a supervisor (for reasons given below) and is given special training on quality circle activities. Alternately, the leader is called a "circle coordinator," although this title is sometimes used for other purposes.
- A quality circle program has a "quality circle facilitator" who is responsible for monitoring, guiding, promoting, coordinating, training and communicating the essentials of quality circle techniques. The facilitator provides an interface between the quality circles and other organizational groups, including a management steering committee.
- A management steering committee establishes objectives, policies and guidelines for quality circle activities and supports the quality circle system through adequate resources and management awareness.

- An optional policy committee oversees the operation of multiple steering committees and determines the overall level of management commitment to the quality circle program.

Thus, a quality circle program is a well-defined set of policies, procedures and people established to increase the effectiveness of the total work environment. The key element in the program is participation, and the basis for participation is knowledge and training. Every participant in a quality circle program—ranging from the circle member to the policy committee director—receives training or familiarization as is appropriate to his or her degree of involvement.

Organization for Quality Circles

No change to the organizational structure is needed to achieve a successful quality circle program. The policy and steering committees represent traditional management functions. Similarly, circle members and leaders assume their normal roles in the organization, supplemented, of course, by quality circle activities. The only new position is the quality circle facilitator, who oversees the operation of several circles. In some organizations, the facilitator is a member of the human resources department—perhaps the Management Development/Organizational Development (MD/OD) staff. In others, the facilitator can be a member of the Education/Training, Operations, or Quality department. In any case, the result is the same. The facilitator works through the existing organization to establish a quality circle program and subsequently makes it possible for the results of quality circle activities to be recognized and integrated into the operational basis of the organization.

Figure 2.1 gives an organizational chart for quality circle activities. At a glance, it is evident that member involvement is crucial to an effective program. Every link in the chain, however—including the development of suitable policies and procedures—is needed for the results of the activities to show benefits for the organization. In fact, an avenue for the implementation and integration of these results must exist through complementary policies and procedures in order for a program to survive. Without effective support, a quality circle program can easily be regarded by circle members as another management attempt to increase productivity without offering tangible resources. Clearly, quality circles should increase productivity by "working smarter," but initially the key factor should be participation.

Figure 2.2 gives a list of conceptual job descriptions in a logical quality circle chain. An optional *coordinator* position—not to be confused with the quality circle leader mentioned earlier—is included as a means of materializing the directives of the steering committee in some organizational settings. In most cases, the directives can easily be handled by the facilitators.

In addition to the primary sources given previously, the facilitator and coordinator positions can

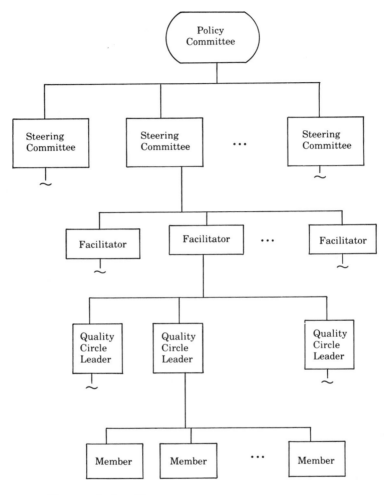

FIGURE 2.1   ORGANIZATION OF QUALITY CIRCLE
ACTIVITIES.

readily be handled by staff assistants in technical areas, such as banking, data processing, and manufacturing. Since a quality circle works from within the organization, any member of the ex-

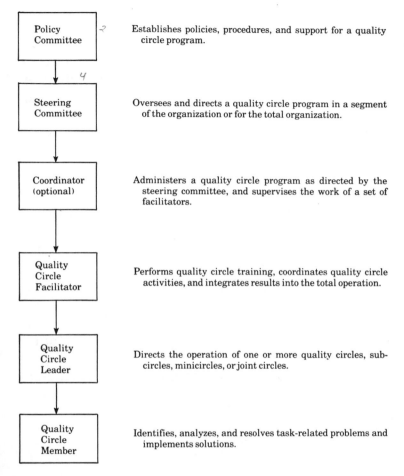

Policy Committee	Establishes policies, procedures, and support for a quality circle program.
Steering Committee	Oversees and directs a quality circle program in a segment of the organization or for the total organization.
Coordinator (optional)	Administers a quality circle program as directed by the steering committee, and supervises the work of a set of facilitators.
Quality Circle Facilitator	Performs quality circle training, coordinates quality circle activities, and integrates results into the total operation.
Quality Circle Leader	Directs the operation of one or more quality circles, subcircles, minicircles, or joint circles.
Quality Circle Member	Identifies, analyzes, and resolves task-related problems and implements solutions.

FIGURE 2.2 LIST OF CONCEPTUAL "JOB DESCRIPTIONS" IN A LOGICAL QUALITY CIRCLE CHAIN.

isting organizational structure (i.e., the department) has a distinct advantage over external personnel in establishing an effective program.

In following sections, a role model is given for each of the participants covered here.

Policy Formulation

The basis for policy formulation is the specification of purposes and thereafter objectives for the program. The purposes of a quality circle program are threefold:

- To enhance the capability of an enterprise to achieve its intended purposes—be it profit, service, or any other form of achievement.
- To provide motivational factors for human fulfillment and to permit the process of participating in work to be a meaningful human experience. In short, this is the process of regarding people as humans and machines as objects and allowing the two modalities to be integrated only when necessary for achieving an intended purpose.
- To fully utilize and expand the capabilities of individuals through training and participation, and by providing a basis for using the innate creativity of people.

Based on these fundamental purposes, a set of objectives can be developed that serve as input to the processes of policy formulation. Objectives are necessary for establishing the operational limits of a policy. While many major and minor objectives can be listed, it is particularly important to present only those that are reasonably independent of management style, organizational structure, and the type of enterprise. Five universal objectives are given:

- To improve productivity and quality
- To improve communications
- To enhance cooperative behavior
- To provide an efficient operation
- To enhance morale

Productivity and *quality* can be achieved through a strong workshop that encourages problem detection, analysis and resolution. Looking at the total picture, workers best know where their productivity can be increased and recognize operations that contribute to lower quality or even poor quality. So, a quality circle program can contribute to high productivity and quality when integrated into the workshop routine.

Effective *communication* is necessary for the foreman, supervisor or manager to achieve a positive influence and a state of control over the employees. It is obviously necessary for a workshop or office to perform in a given way regardless of the enterprise. In a controlled workshop, potential problems are "nipped in the bud" by the observance of established and accepted standards. When appropriate corrective measures are taken with abnormal conditions, causes that would ordinarily result in out-of-control situations are resolved before disastrous effects occur. Control can be achieved through automation—such as the use of industrial robotics—and also by establishing realistic standards and operating procedures.

People cooperate when they understand the job, the requirements and standards, and each other. When people engage in group problem-solving, as with quality circles, they enhance *co-*

operative behavior. Since quality circle activities are voluntary, people cooperate because they want to contribute to their own success. One of management's greatest failings in the post-Theory Y era is the assumption that workers may be loyal and hard-working, but are nevertheless subordinate in their ability to make intellectual contributions in the area of decision-making. Nothing could be farther from the truth, since the workers know their individual jobs and the associated operational environment better than anyone. Moreover, attitudes of this sort (recognizing that they also exist between levels of managing) have a tendency to become a self-fulfilling prophecy. What has been lacking, obviously, is the mechanism for allowing people to contribute, and the use of an effective quality circle program now appears to be the answer.

› A key objective of quality circles is to assist in providing an *efficient operation.* This can be regarded as the same as "productivity and quality," but it can also represent a way of looking at the costs inherent in preventing, appraising, reducing and resolving failure. Failure costs, regardless of whether they reflect service or product failure, can be determined through an effective reporting system. Needed information is obtained by monitoring, analysis, summarization and communication. Monitoring, analysis, and summarization rely on quality circle techniques, and communication is a group process. Through participation, the formulation of the quality measures helps to ensure the success of a program to reduce failures and improve efficiency.

Looking at the enterprise collectively as being composed of management and workers, it has been recognized in the past that quality circles form (or are formed) for three reasons:

- Training
- Problem-solving and generating ideas
- The natural tendency of people with a common interest to band together

It has also been recognized that the overall contribution by workers and foremen to the solution of quality control problems does not extend to more than 15% of the problems. So, why all the fuss over the simple concept of "getting together to solve problems"? The answer is improved *morale* and an increased desire to implement solutions to recognized problems. Potential benefits are evident from the two main ways that quality circles are formed:

- As employees from the same work unit, but not necessarily performing the same task
- As employees performing the same task, such as word processing, in different organizational units

In either case, employees can share work-related problems, resulting in a higher level of effectiveness. Quality circles do not result from high morale; rather, high morale results from quality circles. While quality circles should not be regarded as a management tool for controlling the workplace, a higher level of management control is pragmatically achieved through worker participation.

The set of purposes and objectives feed into a strong policy statement that can give the quality circle program direction and continuity. This approach provides a guide to management activity with regard to:

- Consistency of management action
- Delegation of responsibility
- Uniformity of follow-up

Overall, a good policy structure eliminates confusion and reduces misunderstanding. Because of the diversity of tasks that may be involved and the number of people, the policy should be reasonably short and well-defined. Table 2.1 gives a sample policy that can serve as a "starting place" for any organization initiating a quality circle program.

TABLE 2.1   SAMPLE POLICY FOR QUALITY CIRCLES.

Employee participation:
1. Employees are free to join in, not join in, discontinue, or continue participation in a relevant quality circle.
2. An employee may suggest problems for solution to a relevant quality circle or to management for general solution.

Management support:
3. Management will encourage quality circle membership and participation.
4. Management will provide resources for quality circle activities.
5. Management will publicize quality circle activities.

Management participation:
6. Management will respond to quality circle requests for

information, recommendations, and for management participation.

7. Management will implement approved quality circle solutions.
8. Management will provide training support.

Quality circle activities:

9. Quality circle members will follow techniques and procedures established in the quality circle manual.
10. Quality circle members will recognize the anonymity of members.
11. Quality circle members will respect an employee's voluntary right of participation.
12. Quality circle members collectively have the right to accept or reject problems submitted by management, other circles, or other members.
13. Quality circle members are responsible for identifying, analyzing and implementing problem solutions.
14. Quality circles may submit problems to management for acceptance.
15. Quality circle members will collaborate on work-related problems.
16. Quality circle members will respect the integrity of other circle members.
17. Quality circles will present periodic reviews of activities to management.

Organization:

18. Quality circle organization will consist of an optional policy committee, one or more steering committees, optional coordinators, a facilitator, quality circle leaders, and quality circle members.

Restrictions:

19. Quality circles will not address subjects related to employee complaints, personnel policy, compensation, labor relations, and personal employee problems or characteristics.
20. Management will not penalize or impose restrictions on employees as a result of participation in quality circle activities.

Implementation

The implementation of quality circles is straightforward and practically without risk. In fact, the simplicity of the approach to participative management can easily belie the potential benefits that can be derived. Two similar implementation plans are described in the literature, one by Ingle (1982) and the other by Beardsley (1977). Both can be properly regarded as top-down approaches, since an implicit assumption is made that the overall concept has already been sold to top management. They are summarized, in spite of their similarity, in Tables 2.2 and 2.3.

TABLE 2.2   THE INGLE APPROACH TO
TOP-DOWN IMPLEMENTATION.

Step	Description
1	*Select a two-person team—one from quality control and one from industrial relations.* (The team will do the necessary research and establish the basis for the use of quality circles in the organization.)
2	*Research.* (The team will collect and summarize relevant literature on the subject.)
3	*Attend a seminar.* (The team, as well as other interested parties, should attend an outside seminar, given by experts, on quality circle methods and case studies.)
4	*Observe quality circles.* (Visit an organization that uses quality circles and observe the group dynamics of a circle in operation.)
5	*Decide to start.* (Results are summarized and presented to top management for final approval.)
6	*Select a facilitator.* (This is a key position involved with planning, coordinating, training and follow through.)

7   *Form a steering committee.* (The steering committee provides overall direction for the program and substantiates resource requirements.)

8   *Develop plans and goals.* (Establish objectives, goals, and associated strategic and tactical plans.)

9   *Present the plan to management and the union.* (Communicate the philosophy of quality circle participation and the detailed strategic and tactical plans to all levels of management and pertinent union officials.)

10   *Develop training materials.* (The materials should include presentations, manuals, techniques—a complete scenario for quality circle activities.)

11   *Present the concept to the group.* (The quality circle groups involved in implementation should be consulted and familiarized with the objectives and goals.)

12   *Start training.* (The training plan should be prepared and actual training of members and leaders should be initiated.)

13   *Form circles.* (Working quality circles should be formed in the latter stages of training.)

14   *Review monthly progress.* (A status report covering all quality circle projects should be prepared on a periodic basis.)

An alternate scenario for implementation, of course, is to use a bottom-up approach. A department manager or foreman hears about quality circles and decides to try the idea in a problem area. In some cases, members of the human resources staff can even recommend the concept to managers with quality or personnel problems. As a result, a pilot project is started, preferably with top management's blessing. If good results are obtained, the concept can be dispersed within the organization through a sponsor. Two key advantages of the bottom-up approach is that start-up

TABLE 2.3   THE BEARDSLEY APPROACH TO TOP-DOWN
IMPLEMENTATION.

Step	Description
1	*Discovery.* (A person in the organization experiences a need and relates it to the quality circle concept. At this time, the ideas are reasonably well-known.)
2	*Research.* (Collect reference materials.)
3	*Seminar attendance.* (Attend a seminar given by a specialist on the subject. This step signifies a transition from the research to the implementation stage.)
4	*Witness quality circles in action.* (Visit an organization using quality circles to discuss the concept and observe a circle in operation.)
5	*Decision to start.* (Discuss the quality circle with concerned employees and summarize results for top management's approval.)
6	*Consultation.* (Decide whether an outside consultant is needed to assist in planning, training, and analysis.)
7	*Select a facilitator.* (This person is responsible for coordinating and planning the quality circle program.)
8	*Base-line measurement.* (The "present position" should be recorded in terms of cost, productivity, quality, tardyism, absenteeism, and so forth.)
9	*Create a steering committee.* (A high-level group of staff and management personnel responsible for supporting the program and giving it direction should be formed.)
10	*Develop implementation plan.* (The facilitator, possibly in conjunction with a consultant, develops the general plan for introducing quality circles to the organization. The plan should be coordinated with concerned management and approved by the steering committee.)
11	*Present implementation plan to management.* (The plan should be presented to all levels of management for agreement and familiarization. This step should be supported by the steering committee.)
12	*Develop training materials.* (This involves establishing training objectives, materials, and a realistic plan for ac-

quainting circle leaders and members with quality circle concepts and techniques.)

13 *Conduct leader training class.* (Quality circle leaders are introduced by the facilitator and consultant, if appropriate, to quality circle concepts, methods, and member training. This is an ongoing activity.)

14 *Start the quality circle.* (This involves the preparation of quality circle activities in designated areas, and includes scheduling, personnel selection, planning and notification.

15 *Introduction to potential members.* (This is the "kick-off session" to acquaint circle members with the reasons and objectives in forming a quality circle. This meeting is held by the quality circle leader with the assistance of the facilitator and a "key" management person.)

16 *Conduct member training.* (Circle members are trained in quality circle activities in three or four sessions by the facilitator and leader. In the fourth or fifth meeting, training is tapered off and the group begins to identify, analyze and solve practical problems.)

17 *Program review.* (Quality circle activities should be reviewed periodically by the steering committee, top management, and the policy group.)

costs are lower than with the top-down approach and it is less likely to give the impression that it is another management strategy to increase worker output.

Quality Circle Participants

Four classes of employees participate directly in quality circle operations:

- Steering committee
- Facilitator

- Circle leaders
- Circle members

It is important to note that as the results of quality circle activities affect the organization, management and nonmember employees are also affected. Clearly, when the results of quality circle activities are accepted and implemented by management, the organization must change. However, the very presence of ongoing quality circle activities also changes the operational dimension of the organization through "people building" creativity, team spirit, and the training inherent in the various processes.

STEERING COMMITTEE

From an organizational perspective, a quality circle program cannot succeed without the support of a steering committee. Local solutions to particular management problems can be developed through participative management, but their overall impact will be less than if a total quality circle program is adopted. On the other hand, an overzealous domination by the steering committee of quality circle activities can easily kill an otherwise successful program. So, management must walk a tightrope between the two extremes with frequent adjustments to changing conditions. The greatest danger, mentioned previously, is the possibility that prospective circle members will jump to the conclusion that quality circles are just another management "trick" and will decline to participate. Therefore, the committee must give careful attention to the policies that will guide circle participation and operation.

The steering committee should include staff personnel as well as managers from the broad spectrum of organizational functions. Rather than "make it happen," the steering committee's maxim should be "let it happen."

Table 2.4 gives a summarization of quality circle functions. Other than administrative tasks, the committee should focus on objectives, areas of concentration, personnel assignments, and overall operation of the program. Union participation should be encouraged but not expected. Some unions prefer to observe rather than participate. It is important that quality circle activities do not overlap union jurisdiction, and a policy to this effect is normally established.

The size of the steering committee is not as important as the fact that it represents the total organization and meets regularly. Specialists indicate that a minimum membership of five and a maximum of fifteen is ideal.

In small organizations (or small quality circle programs), the facilitator should be a member of the steering committee. For large programs, this is clearly impossible because several facilitators would normally be needed.

Training of the steering committee is minimal but important. Policies and day-to-day operations are largely dependent upon a particular organization, so a briefing on quality circle concepts is all that is normally needed. A consultant, the sponsor, or an experienced facilitator can easily perform the briefing. It follows that familiarization

TABLE 2.4 STEERING COMMITTEE FUNCTIONS.

- Develops policies and guidelines
- Establishes a regular monthly meeting time
- Identifies to whom the steering committee will report
- Prepares objectives and prepares implementation plan to achieve these objectives
- Provides guidance and direction
- Determines funding arrangements
- Determines areas on which circles can focus attention
- Promulgates quality circles throughout the organization
- Identifies milestones in circle progress
- Determines or reviews start-dates of circles
- Identifies and approves leaders for circles
- Establishes qualifications for facilitators
- Decides on frequency of circle meetings
- Decides how divisions and departments will learn about quality circles
- Schedules familiarization presentations and orientations
- Selects facilitators
- Establishes how efforts of circles will be recognized and re-warded (if appropriate)
- Periodically reviews program milestones
- Attends management presentations (of quality circle activity)
- Meets periodically with facilitators

should be informal in line with the key objective of participative management.

The chairman of the steering committee can be appointed by top management, can be elected, or can be a member of top management itself. In any case, the person should be democratic, open to suggestion, and definitely not a "table-pounder." Nothing can kill a quality circle program more quickly than a dominating steering committee, and a domineering leader can severely influence the committee in that direction. In his or her own way, the chairman of the steering committee has to be a salesperson to counteract the negativism normally associated with something new. Two aspects of selling are required: selling on the merits of the program and selling to obtain involvement. Many managers do not want to be guinea pigs and feel comfortable with historical methods—even though the methods may be largely ineffective.

There are also some management decisions associated with the steering committee's activities. Most decisions relate to the facilitator and involve selection and full-time vs. part-time participation. Policies for selecting leaders and establishing recognition and rewards are also significant.

FACILITATOR

The facilitator is the key person in a results-oriented quality circle program. He promotes the quality circle concept and coordinates the activities of leaders, the steering committee, and management. The facilitator coordinates within circles and among circles and serves as the interface to other departments, such as engineering or marketing. When assistance is needed from outside groups, he arranges it. The facilitator reports to management and the steering committee on the status of the quality circle program in the organi-

TABLE 2.5   FACILITATOR FUNCTIONS.

- Trains leaders
- Promotes the quality circle program to employees, supervisors, middle and upper management
- Believes completely in quality circles as a method of developing employee potential
- Promotes, implements, operates and manages a quality circle program
- Motivates, supports and encourages people
- Sets standards and priorities
- Optionally participates in steering committee activities

zation. Facilitator functions are summarized in Table 2.5.

The facilitator serves also as a trainer for quality circle leaders and possibly for circle members. In essence, he embodies quality circle expertise which is manifested through the preparation of training materials and promotional literature.

The facilitator effectively sets quality circle standards for the organization and is knowledgeable of analysis techniques and methods of presentation.

Personal qualifications of a successful facilitator vary widely depending upon the parent organization. Overall, however, he is a people-oriented person, challenged by the process of working through people to get the job done. While the facilitator need not be a manager, the pay scale for the position should be roughly equivalent to that of a technical employee.

There are two basic prerequisites for this position: coordination experience and a background in the primary function of the organization, such as manufacturing or banking. The facilitator should have the personality to "get out and mingle with the people." He should believe in the quality circle concept and have the ability to instill the same enthusiasm in leaders and members.

The facilitator is normally responsible for a number of quality circles, and in large organizations with an extensive program, several facilitators may report to a senior facilitator. In the latter case, the senior facilitator should sit on the steering committee.

CIRCLE LEADER

The circle leader is responsible for the operation of one quality circle and works closely with the facilitator in establishing the circle and training the members. He has essentially the same training as the facilitator without the same span of control. In fact, the facilitator and circle leader may work closely in member training and collaborate during the sessions.

The circle leader will frequently be the group's supervisor, although this need not necessarily be the case. Initially, it is a good idea to start with the supervisor as leader, provided that the members accept the arrangement. Usually, the supervisor has the breadth of experience to ensure that the circle goes in the right direction. Later, he can continue as leader or the group can elect one of the other members as the leader. In any case, the supervisor should participate in the circle's operation.

Another consideration is that the supervisor is

more likely to get ideas accepted by top management because a certain level of credibility already exists.

One approach to establishing the circle leader is to have the supervisor hold this position, and after a period of circle operation, to appoint a member as assistant leader. Eventually, the assistant can evolve into the full leader. It is also possible to elect the initial leader from within the group, but this approach tends to leave the supervisor dangling with nothing to do.

Table 2.6 gives a representative set of quality circle leader functions. Clearly, all are significant, but perhaps the most important function is that the leader is responsible for the operation of the circle. Problem selection, analysis, data collection, participation and discussion, and problem-solving are all under direct control of the quality circle leader. When participation wanes through a lack of challenging ideas, the leader initiates brainstorming to generate new ones. When members experience difficulty in communicating and getting their contributions recognized, the leader assists through encouragement and diplomacy. Finally, the leader is responsible for winding up a topic and for fostering its acceptance by management.

A circle leader may also participate in a leader circle that has the objective of applying participative management to the quality circle program itself. It is here that leader methodology is exchanged among circle leaders. Some of the topics that frequently arise are policies, codes of conduct, organization, scheduling and training.

TABLE 2.6 QUALITY CIRCLE LEADER FUNCTIONS.

- Trains members with assistance from the facilitator as needed
- Responsible for circle activities
- Responsible for the operation of the circle
- Assists with circle reporting andhe circle
- Prepares the agenda for circle meetings
- Enforces policies and rules of conduct
- Assists in analysis and problem-solving

Several procedural items can assist in making a quality circle program run smoothly from the standpoint of the circle leader:

- Start and end meetings on time
- Plan the meetings in advance
- Prepare, distribute and use an agenda
- Summarize meetings for the next session
- Document results
- Use a critique session to enhance performance
- Control the discussion process so members stay on the right track and work towards an objective of problem identification, analysis, or solution

In addition, the leader must train members, and these sessions occupy the first few circle meetings. After the methodology is presented, meetings evolve into a problem-solving modality. While responsibility for the smooth and effective operation of a quality circle is that of the circle leader, the facilitator provides support as long as it is needed.

The facilitator attends early meetings, but this form of participation diminishes over time.

CIRCLE MEMBERS

The objective of the quality circle philosophy is to enlist the participation of circle members drawn from an object department. Even though membership is voluntary and a certain amount of freedom exists as far as joining, leaving, and then rejoining a circle by members is concerned, there should be a genuine effort on the part of management, the union, the facilitator, and the circle leader to encourage total participation. As a "person building" technique, the benefits of quality circle participation should be available to all employees. (Nowadays, employees are concerned with career paths. Well, a career path without participation management experience is like engineering without mathematics. In short, you can't get along without it.)

Quality circle members are trained by their circle leader who is often assisted by the facilitator. Members take training to learn the techniques and to gain familiarity with circle operations and group dynamics. Towards the end of the training period, the group attacks real problems in the workplace. Initially, quality circle problems are proposed by management, the facilitator, and the circle leader. Later, members propose problems on their own.

Table 2.7 summarizes the functions of circle members. Members should all do the same kind

TABLE 2.7   CIRCLE MEMBER FUNCTIONS.

- Attends periodic meetings
- Adheres to circle policies and code of conduct
- Learns and applies quality circle methods
- Participates in problem identification, analysis and solution
- Participates in management presentations
- Encourages participation of other members and nonmembers

of work, or at least work on the same problem. Quality circles formed as a combination of specialists—such as electricians, machinists, and plumbers—often discourage participation because some specialists are invariably observing while others are working on a problem. In general, it is best if members of a given quality circle report to the same supervisor. When specialists are needed during problem-solving, they can be brought in by the facilitator.

Casey Stengel was quoted as saying, "The game's not over until it's over." In a similar vein, the key to participative management is participation. Accordingly members should:

- Attend all meetings
- Actively engage in solving problems
- Follow the code of conduct

The *code of conduct* for circle members, given in Table 2.8, is nothing but common sense and ordinary courtesy. It helps to have the code contained in the training materials.

TABLE 2.8   CODE OF CONDUCT FOR CIRCLE MEMBERS.

- Each member should attend all meetings
- Each member should participate
- Members may criticize ideas but not people
- Each member is free to express ideas or make suggestions
- Members should listen to contributions of others
- Members should work on a group project

Operation of a Quality Circle

The two key aspects of quality circle operation are training and problem-solving. During the start-up phase, training is the main activity, and the first two or three sessions are devoted exclusively to that subject. After problem-solving has begun, training proceeds on a topical basis as new techniques become necessary to resolve new situations.

Problems are suggested by management, the facilitator, the circle leader, or through member participation. The latter case normally takes the form of a brainstorming session or an idea thought of by a member and communicated to the group. Realistically, most problems attacked by a quality circle are commonly associated with the everyday workplace; only rarely do quality circle problems approach interdepartmental affairs or affect the organization as a whole. Yet, small problems may lead to big troubles, especially if they are compounded.

The operation of a quality circle takes place through the following steps:

- Problem identification
- Problem selection (by members)
- Problem-solving (by members)
- Recommendation to management
- Management review of recommendation
- Decision by management

The problem-solving phase is commonly augmented by specialists and with information from other areas of the organization.

While the steps appear to be self-evident, their individual processes may be less obvious. For example, a typical quality problem experienced in manufacturing is the production of parts that are out of tolerance. Call this a *result problem*. There are usually many causes, each of which can be a potential problem to be solved by circle members. Data collection and analysis may be necessary to identify the primary causes, and only then do the members select a *cause problem* to solve. Usually, the major cause problem is solved by the circle, but this is not always possible. It is conceivable that the major cause of problems is interdepartmental or industry-wide. Systems problems of this type require more than a quality circle—perhaps a task force. Also, some industry-wide problems are accepted by all persons involved. A quality circle would then attack an appropriate subproblem for solution.

In spite of the wide diversity of problem situations, an analysis procedure seems to be the most amenable and common to one or more of the phases. The following steps to the analysis procedure have been proposed in a variety of forms:

1. Plan (P)
2. Collect data (C)
3. Analyze data (A)
4. Draw conclusions (D)

The analysis procedure is a subject of Chapter III.

Once a cause to a result problem has been identified, it becomes a problem in and of itself. Circle members, because of their experience with the subject matter, may have an immediate solution. More often than not, however, there may be different and possibly conflicting solutions. Discussion will ensue and eventually a consensus will be reached as to the most appropriate course of action. An implementation plan should be prepared at this point and the solution should be tested before a decision is made by the circle members to make a recommendation to management. Clearly, the P-C-A-D procedure may apply in this case, as well.

The recommendation to management is made through a presentation and possibly a written report, or a description in some form of the problem statement and recommended solution.

The management presentation—set up by the facilitator—is no small undertaking. Charts and possibly slides must be prepared, and several walkthroughs of the presentation may be needed. The presentation should not be made to the steering committee but to the manager to whom the circle leader reports. Clearly, high-level management may sit in—and this is obviously recommended. However, the review process should parallel the formal organization structure; bypassing the normal control structure could easily lead to negative results.

The management review and eventual decision should take place in a reasonable time period. Actually, it is preferable to make the time of the review period a matter of policy. Otherwise, the circle may not be responsive to the next problem that surfaces.

Varieties of Quality Circles

The dynamics of quality circle activities frequently lead to problems or subproblems that are either too big, too small, or too specialized for the group. In some cases, a major problem is caused by several subproblems, each of which is best handled by a select group under the leadership of a knowledgeable member. In other cases, a problem may be too small for a 12-person group to attack and can be assigned to a subgroup. In a sense, "Too many cooks . . ." Not only do minicircles increase the sense of participation among members, but they also permit a sharper focus on a problem than is possible with a larger group.

In an analogous vein, quality circles also grow in experience, competence, and their ability to attempt more sophisticated problems. Often, problems span different shops, each of which has an ongoing quality circle. When problems span shops, departments, and offices, *joint quality circles* can be formed to solve common problems. Normally, they involve shops, one of which precedes the other in a manufacturing or commercial process.

As quality circle members become familiar with more analysis techniques and gain experience in the problem-solving process, mini and joint quality circles are a natural consequence. *Leader circles* are commonplace, and even *facilitator circles* have been initiated.

Success Elements

The elements that lead to a successful quality circle program are integral to many of the topics covered previously, such as voluntary participation and management support. In fact, dozens of books exist on motivation, human relations, communication, learning, and management. Nevertheless, there are ten critical success factors that stand out and should be seriously considered before a quality circle plan is put into effect. Overall, they serve as a "success check list":

1. Effective leadership
2. Attention to rewards and recognition
3. Linkage to the suggestion system
4. Attention to group processes
5. Adequate training
6. Realistic goals
7. Well-defined roles and expectations
8. Promotional activities
9. Efficient recordkeeping
10. Careful measurement and testing

These critical success factors can be used by top management to oversee the quality circle program and should definitely be used by the steering committee and facilitators to gauge progress. Attention to the success factors coupled with an ongoing plan for monitoring, assessment, and control will lead to a successful program.

Summary

A quality circle is a small group of workers who meet regularly on a voluntary basis to analyze problems and recommend solutions to management. The organizational sphere of activity of quality circle participants is the area in which they work. The basic philosophy underlying quality circles is that quality awareness through participative management can not only identify problem situations but can also assist management in solving them. Some quality circle attributes are:

- Participation is voluntary
- A quality circle is a small group ranging from four to twelve people
- Quality circle members do similar work
- Quality circles meet regularly
- Each quality circle has a formal leader
- A quality circle program in an organization has one or more facilitators that guide the program
- A management steering committee establishes objectives, policies and guidelines for the program

Each participant in a quality circle program receives adequate training to enhance his involvement.

No organizational change is needed to implement a quality circle program, but a successful program will most certainly change the organization. The key participants in a program are:

- The steering committee
- Facilitator
- Circle leaders
- Circle members

All participants, other than the facilitator, are drawn from the existing workforce. The facilitator is a new position that may be staffed from manufacturing, industrial engineering, or the human resources department.

The basis for quality circle policy formulation is the specification of purposes and objectives for the problem. Key purposes are:

- To enhance the capability of the enterprise
- To provide motivational factors
- To fully utilize and expand the capabilities of individuals

Based on these purposes, five universal objectives of a quality circle program are:

- To improve productivity and quality
- To improve communications
- To enhance cooperative behavior
- To provide an efficient operation
- To enhance morale

The two main ways that quality circles are formed are as employees from the same work unit, but not necessarily performing the same task, and as employees performing the same task—such as word processing—in different organizational units. Accordingly, the major elements of a quality circle policy are:

- Employee participation
- Management support
- Management participation
- Quality circle activities
- Organization
- Restrictions

The implementation of quality circles can proceed on a top-down or bottom-up basis. Top-down implementation refers to a total program initiated by top management and affecting the whole organization. Bottom-up implementation refers to the pilot project approach that is expanded as conditions and needs become evident. In either case, a successful program requires a sponsor to foster the concepts. The steps in quality circle implementation are well-defined.

The operation of a quality circle takes place through the following steps:

- Problem identification
- Problem selection (by members)
- Problem-solving (by members)
- Recommendation to management
- Management review of recommendation
- Decision by management

The problem-solving phase is commonly augmented by specialists and with information from other areas of the organization. An analysis procedure inherent in several of the above steps seems to be the most amenable to routinization. The following steps to the analysis procedure have been proposed in a variety of forms:

1. Plan (P)
2. Collect data (C)
3. Analyze data (A)
4. Draw conclusions (D)

In general, two types of problems exist: result problems and cause problems. A quality circle solves a result problem—such as excessive operating costs—by analyzing and dividing it into subproblems—such as telephone utilization and outside services—through quality circle techniques, and then solving major subproblems through quality circle activities. Major problems can be divided into subproblems to be handled by minicircles, and problems that span shops or departments can be handled by joint quality circles.

III

QUALITY CIRCLE METHODS

Introduction

Some organizations with long experience in participative management, in management development/organizational development programs, and in quality assurance can use the top-down approach to quality circle implementation and have the resources to buffer the costs until positive results are received. Not all are convinced, however, that a quality circle program will be successful in their organization. In this case, the most prudent approach is to initiate a pilot project and then measure the results. If results are favorable, then the program can be extended into other areas. Otherwise, the program can be discontinued or initiated in another area. On the other hand, there could be an even more important reason to measure results from quality circle activities. An effective measurement program can justify continuation of a quality circle program when political winds change and a new administration is not convinced of a program's viability. At the quality circle level, measurement and analysis techniques are used for problem identification, problem analysis, problem solution, and to support recommendations to management. This chapter covers measurement, data collection, and methods that are applied to collected data. In the latter area, statistics, cause-and-effect diagrams, and Pareto diagrams are discussed. Brainstorming is covered as a method for problem identification and analysis.

Measurement

The measurement techniques used to support, justify and analyze the operations of a quality circle program are essentially no different than any other techniques. Since quality circle members, as a general rule, want to exhibit good results, they characteristically have a good attitude towards measurement. Measurements can be grouped into three categories: quality indicators, cost analysis, and attitude indicators.

QUALITY INDICATORS

Clearly, *quality indicators* differ between production shops and service industries. Nevertheless, similarities are evidenced by the representative set of quality indicators given in Table 3.1.

Indicators are not always obvious. In a data processing shop, for example, errors due to mounting the wrong tape were counted and analyzed at daily meetings. Shrewd computer operators, however, determined that reruns of the same job were

TABLE 3.1   REPRESENTATIVE QUALITY INDICATORS.

Billing errors	Recalls
Breakdowns	Repeat purchasing
Contract errors	Repeated errors
Customer complaints	Repeated failures
Customer rejections	Reruns
Defects	Review-based actions
Defects per unit of work	Rework costs
Delays due to errors	Scrap levels
Design changes	Shortages
Late deliveries	Spoilage
Lawsuits	Time lost due to breakdowns
Methods improvement	Tool rework
Process changes	Warranty claims
Purchase order changes	Yield rate

not recorded. So, when an incorrect tape was mounted, they allowed the job to run to completion, and then reran it with the correct tape. This quality system literally wasted thousands of hours of valuable computer time.

One way of looking at quality indicators is to draw a chart, as shown in Figure 3.1. In 3.1(a), the causes are organized with regard to frequency, which gives one a picture of the quality situation. The most frequent cause is placed first, the second most frequent cause is placed next, and so forth. In terms of cost, as in 3.1(b), quite a different result is obtained. In this case, causes are arranged according to the cost impact on the organization.

In many organizations, workers can easily cover-up errors and there are no means of measuring reruns, recalls, and customer inconvenience—

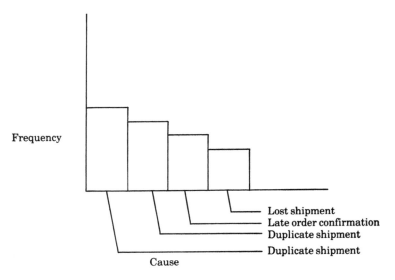

(a) Arranged by frequency

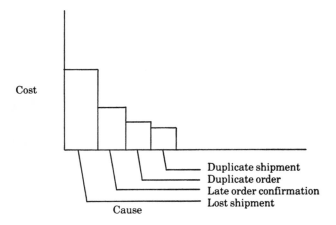

(b) Arranged by cost

FIGURE 3.1   ANALYSIS OF QUALITY INDICATORS.

except at the bottom line. Through quality circle activities, many sources of poor quality are uncovered through the normal processes of group dynamics. Thus, it is realistic to contend that quality circles work *with* measurement techniques, rather than stating that one technique is dependent upon the others.

COST ANALYSIS

Cost figures are the language of production shops and service industries. Therefore, any cost reduction achieved through quality circle activities is relative to the corresponding cost level. One measure commonly used is the savings-to-cost ratio. When an improvement is recommended in a procedure or process, the costs and savings are projected into the future to give a realistic picture of the value of the suggestion.

All quality improvements can be translated into either cost reductions or productivity gains. Production people have a variety of methods for projecting production and cost data to estimate the payback or improved cash flow of a proposed scheme. Perhaps the most powerful and easily understood of these methods is the learning curve (commonly associated with motor learning in humans). The key to the learning curve, as applied to production, is that the rate of improvement (or *gain*) in a process is sufficiently well-defined to be predictable. This is the case because of familiarization and the experience of personnel, adjustments to and fine-tuning of equipment, enhanced man-machine interaction, enhanced processing flow, and improved design methods so that products are *designed* to be manufactured in addition to being designed for hard use.

The learning curve implies that production tends to improve by a constant percentage each time production doubles. Figure 3.2 depicts a learning curve at a percentage of 80%. This means that the second 1,000 units require only 80% of the resources as do the first 1,000 units, and so forth.

Implicit in the learning curve is the underlying assumption that an active ongoing attempt is

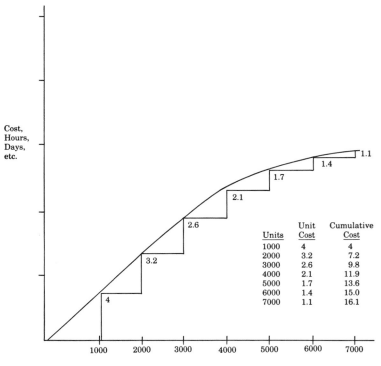

FIGURE 3.2 PRODUCTION LEARNING CURVE (RATE = 80%).

made to improve the process. This is precisely the case with a quality circle program. After recommendations are made and accepted by top management, quality circle activity continues. New problems are continually identified, analyzed and resolved. In time, as a matter of fact, it is conceivable that new recommendations will supersede older ones as environmental conditions change.

ATTITUDE INDICATORS

Many organizations are adept at measuring production and service data, but have limited experience with the measurement of employee attitudes. While the items to be measured seem to be obvious, once they are mentioned, many people simply have not thought about them. This is probably the case because they haven't had to do it or didn't think it was important. Well, employee attitudes *are* important, and a quality circle program can significantly improve employee motivation through participative management. Attitudes can be improved even if they are already good. There is no need to describe attitude indicators but to simply list them:

- Employee absences
- Tardiness
- Grievances
- Turnover
- Attitude surveys
- Direct observation

For absences, tardiness, grievances and turnover, personnel records are a satisfactory source of information. Attitude surveys and direct observation require "human resource" training and experience, although some organizations may want to handle the measurements informally.

Measurement, in the sense of this section, refers to the evaluation of a quality circle program. General guidelines for the measurements of a quality circle program are normally determined by the organization's strategic plan.

Brainstorming

In the dynamics of quality circle activities, ideas are needed to identify problems, uncover probable causes, and develop viable solutions. A commonly-used technique to stimulate ideas in cases such as these is brainstorming.

BASIC CONCEPT

Brainstorming is a group technique for generating ideas. The basic philosophy underlying it is that a response by one person seems to stimulate the creativity of other participants. Often, ideas are held back by a person for a variety of reasons:

- The idea doesn't seem relevant.
- The person is cautious in presenting an idea for fear of being ridiculed.
- The person is not exactly sure that his or her input is wanted.
- The idea is dormant and the right stimulus to cause it to surface is needed.

The reason that brainstorming is successful with quality circle activities is that the group is involved with the work environment that they know best—their own.

Brainstorming is a means of generating the maximum number of ideas on a topic. The brainstorming procedure works as follows:

1. The topic is introduced and the scope of the desired input is clearly stated.
2. The guidelines of brainstorming are briefly reviewed, just to be sure. (This topic will have been covered in the circle members' training program.)
3. Each participant, in turn, is asked for an idea.
4. The ideas are listed on a flip chart or a chalkboard by the circle leader. (The leader may have to summarize an idea with the originator's agreement.)
5. Members are solicited for ideas in rotation until all input is exhausted.

After as many relevant ideas as possible are generated, the circle leader, with the help of the members, goes through an analysis phase to identify the top ideas.

In some cases, an insufficient number of ideas is generated on a topic and the session can be suspended until the next meeting. An incubation period is sometimes beneficial since a successful session is dependent upon the fact that the members are actively familiar with the topic and the proper stimuli are present. By "sleeping on a problem" for a week or two, members have a chance to "wake up" to a problem, cause or solution.

GUIDELINES

Adherence to recognized guidelines can greatly increase the yield of a brainstorming session. The worst thing that can happen is to have members "clam up" because they or someone else has been criticized or laughed at. Also, it may take a considerable amount of courage for some people to give an idea, and these are precisely the ideas that are desired.

The guidelines are simple but effective:

- Each member may offer only one idea per turn.
- The ideas are not discussed. Clarification, if necessary, is permitted, and the idea is then recorded in summarized form.
- Criticism and judgment are not permitted.
- Informality, good-naturedness, laughter and free-wheeling are encouraged. Wild off-beat ideas can trigger a really useful concept. Members are more creative when the atmosphere is not tense and formal.
- Strive for "quantity" of ideas. Quality can come later.
- Encourage improvements to ideas and combinations of ideas.

The biggest problem that the circle leader has is to keep the session on the subject. In spite of its informality, a brainstorming session is not for social purposes. The circle leader must reinforce the fact that the process is quite serious.

The members should also be encouraged not to be ego-involved with an idea. With an improvement upon an idea or a combination of them, a team member can easily get the impression that his or her idea was "stolen." Members should be constantly reminded that quality circle activity is a team process, and also that other members are well aware of where an idea came from—even if they do not say it.

ANALYSIS OF IDEAS

Ideas must be discussed, analyzed and judged. Clearly, "off the wall" ideas must be discarded and sound ideas should be reinforced.

The task of narrowing down the list of ideas is done by voting. Team members are allowed to vote on each idea in turn, and the ideas with the most votes are entered into a discussion phase.

At this point, team members can concentrate their attention on a smaller number of items, where thorough and exhaustive discussion is needed and encouraged. After the discussion period, which may extend to two or more sessions, a final vote is taken on the remaining ideas.

Afterwards, study groups, minicircles, joint quality circles, and data collection and analysis transpire before a final recommendation to management is prepared.

Data Collection

In manufacturing and other forms of commerce, a large amount of data is collected to form the basis for decisions and actions. Reasons for collecting data can be conveniently grouped into the following categories:

- To assist in understanding the situation
- To serve as a basis for analysis of cause-and-effect
- To provide a basis for regulating the process
- To support statistical quality control
- To establish a basis for financial analysis

In most cases, the reporting aspect of data collection is taken for granted, and in many forward-looking organizations, only exception data is reported in order to cut down on the volume of paper required for decision-making and control. It is assumed throughout that the data collected represents the facts and that the analysis is appropriate to the problem domain. Accordingly, sampling and statistical analysis constitute the foundation of data collection.

There are essentially two aspects of data collection that must be considered—recording data and its presentation. The *recording* phase accumulates raw data, and the *method of presentation* is used to display the data in a form that is readily understandable. Clearly, these are both broad topics that can only be introduced here. Moreover, quality circle activities do not in general require advanced methods, and straightforward and easily-understood techniques for recording and presentation are more than satisfactory for most applications.

RECORDING COLLECTED DATA

Data must be recorded for it to be useful for quality circle activities. Four methods are used frequently enough in this area to be mentioned:

1. A check list
2. A drawing
3. A check sheet
4. A computer printout

A *check list* is simply a list of actions performed or items to be inspected. It specifies two items of information: a tabulation of entries (i.e., actions or items) and an implicit order in which the entries should be considered. As an example, a check list could reflect an inspection record wherein various conditions are either accepted or rejected. Another type of check list could simply denote the presence of a certain defect or failure.

Another means of recording data, especially in the quality assurance area, is to denote the existence of a defect on an artistic or mechanical *drawing* for the product. This form could be used to represent flaws in sheetmetal or paintwork, such that the area of greatest susceptibility is signified by the density of marks.

The most frequently used form of recording is the *check sheet*, as suggested by Figure 3.3. On one axis, an event—such as a quality problem—is outlined. On the other axis, a domain—such as a product model—is represented. Thus, occurrences of various events for specified products can be signified by a tabulation mark. The key advan-

Product

	Model A	Model B	Model C	Model D	Total by Quality Problem
Door Molding	卌		//||	||	11
Sheetmetal	////	||	卌	/	12
Paint Finish	卌 //	卌	卌 //||	||||	25
Alignment	//	/	/	//	6
Driveability	卌 ||	卌	卌 /	)|||	22
Total by Product	25	13	25	13	76

(Quality Problem)

FIGURE 3.3   REPRESENTATIVE CHECK SHEET FOR RECORDING DATA.

tage is that the marks can be totaled by event and also by product. The check sheet method also serves as an excellent input to the presentation phase.

The final method of recording covered here is the *computer printout*. Many processes in modern business are controlled by computers. Process-control computers, various forms of automation, data entry stations, and banking terminals are typical examples. Data recording is a by-product of such operations, and errors are tabulated, summarized and reported for management review. This is an excellent source of information provided that the computer output can be produced in a useful format.

Finally, some thought should be given to the process of recording. Some of the usual considerations are the time period for collection, the kind of data to be collected, and format design in the case of check lists, drawings and check sheets. Sampling is a key issue in data collection, and many quality circle groups rely on expert advice from the quality control or industrial engineering departments in this regard.

PRESENTATION OF COLLECTED DATA

The most common method of presentation utilizes a graph that gives a visual model of the concept being presented. An arbitrary distinction is made here between the presentation of collected data and the presentation of analysis data. In the former case, the following are used:

- Line graphs
- Histograms
- Pie charts
- Control charts

In the latter case, two methods prevail:

- Pareto diagrams
- Cause-and-effect diagrams

The Pareto and cause-and-effect diagrams are introduced in the next section. In the final section, the methods are combined as they would be in quality circle analysis.

A *line graph* is normally used to represent collected data summarized over time, as suggested by Figure 3.4. A line graph does not automatically

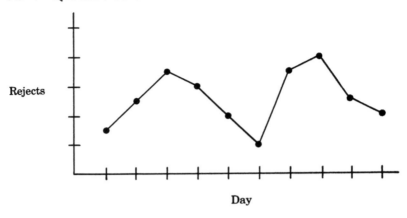

FIGURE 3.4   A REPRESENTATIVE LINE GRAPH.

engender any corrective action on the part of employees or a quality circle because causes are not obvious from data. In fact, a line graph may be generated in response to a quality circle's request for data. It follows that brainstorming or another analysis technique would be used to identify causes and possible solutions.

Closely related to a line graph is the *control chart*, shown in Figure 3.5, on which upper and

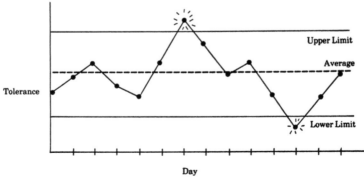

FIGURE 3.5   A REPRESENTATIVE CONTROL CHART.

lower control limits are drawn. Usually, an average value of a variable—such as a tolerance—is recorded versus time. When a periodic value falls outside of the specified range, an investigation into the cause(s) is automatically triggered. As with line graphs, the application of brainstorming or another analysis technique is needed to identify causes and possible solutions.

A *histogram* is a visual diagram in which frequencies are represented by the height of a vertical bar, as shown in Figure 3.6. A slight variation to the frequency histogram is the percentage

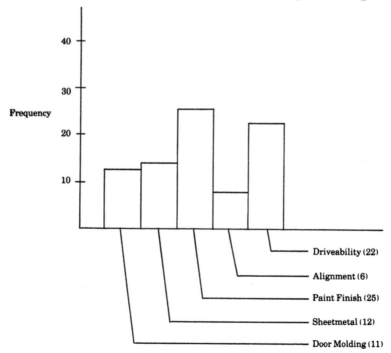

FIGURE 3.6 A REPRESENTATIVE HISTOGRAM (CAUSE VERSUS FREQUENCY).

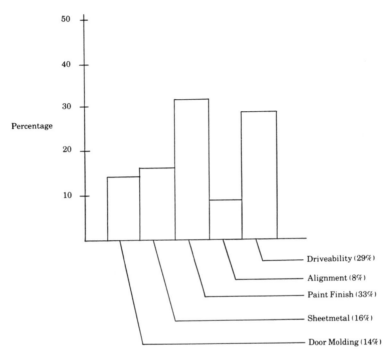

FIGURE 3.7 A REPRESENTATIVE HISTOGRAM (CAUSE VERSUS PERCENTAGE).

histogram, as shown in Figure 3.7, where percentages instead of frequencies are depicted. The shape is the same in either case, so each is an analog of the other. A histogram is used in quality circle activities to identify problems for group solution. In Figure 3.6, for example, the major quality problems are "paint finish" and "driveability." If these major problems were resolved, the quality picture would be considerably different.

A final method for presenting collected data is the *pie chart*, shown in Figure 3.8. This is yet an-

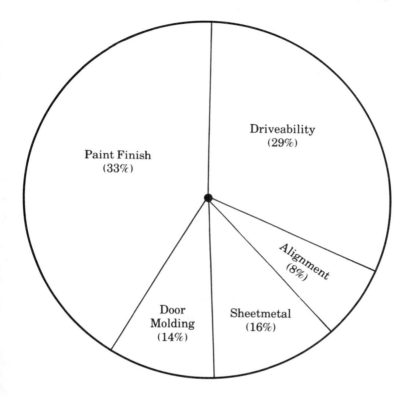

FIGURE 3.8   A REPRESENTATIVE PIE CHART.

other technique for representing frequency and percentage data and is directly analogous to the histogram technique.

Selection among the various methods is largely arbitrary.

ADVANCED METHODS

Additional methods for presenting collected data are scatter diagrams, project charts, and pictograms. Applicable statistical techniques are stratification and correlation. A basic book on applied statistics would be useful for reviewing these methods.

DISCUSSION

Quality circle methods are relatively simple and straightforward because they reflect an attempt to match methodology with the experience level of the participants. Training is problematical since it is impossible to devote more than an hour to a topic in any one session, and this amounts to no more than a brief glimpse at theory, procedures, examples, an exercise, and review questions. Advanced techniques are within the domain of systems analysis, industrial engineers, and quality control specialists.

Data Analysis

Data analysis techniques facilitate the process of identifying problems, causes and solutions and for presenting recommendations to management. Two basic methods are used in quality circle work: Pareto diagrams and cause-and-effect diagrams. The latter are further classed as "basic cause-and-effect" and "process cause-and-effect."

PARETO DIAGRAMS

A Pareto diagram is a means of establishing and visualizing a priority among problems or causes.

It is nothing more than a basic histogram for which the tallest column is placed to the left and the remaining columns are arranged in descending order. Figure 3.9 represents the quality data (originally shown in Figure 3.6) as a Pareto diagram. It is obvious, in this case, that the major quality problem is "paint finish," such that even a partial reduction of causes of this problem would produce more satisfactory results than eliminating another problem.

The combination of a line graph with a Pareto

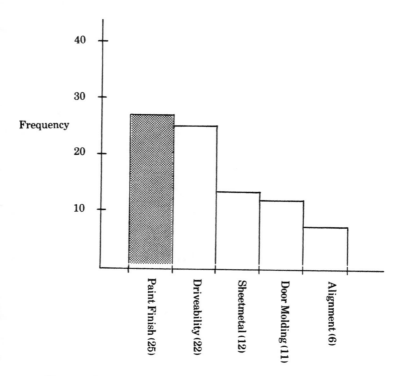

FIGURE 3.9   A REPRESENTATIVE PARETO DIAGRAM.

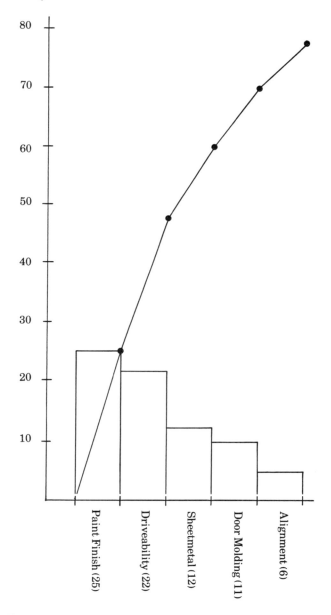

FIGURE 3.10 "Cum" LINE ON A PARETO DIAGRAM.

diagram produces a cumulative or "cum" line, as shown in Figure 3.10. The cum line is constructed as follows:

- Starting at zero, the cum line is extended to the upper right-hand corner of the leftmost column.
- The cum line is then extended by the height of the second column to a point directly above the right-hand edge of the column.
- The process is continued for remaining columns.

The cum line is complete when it represents 100% of the cases.

The combination of a cum line with a Pareto diagram is ideal for management presentations, as shown in Figure 3.11, because it graphically depicts a gain made through quality circle activities. In this case, a quality control improvement was made to "paint finish," reducing the number of problems from 25 to 10. It should be noted that the position of the improved column is also shifted.

As noted previously, a variation to a Pareto diagram is to represent the "cost of quality" associated with various quality problems, instead of frequencies or percentages. This gives an alternate view of cost reduction and can shift priorities markedly.

BASIC CAUSE-AND-EFFECT

When a problem (i.e., an effect) is known and its causes are not known, an excellent group technique for problem analysis is to construct a cause-

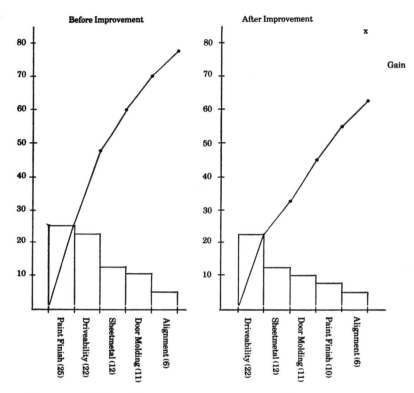

FIGURE 3.11 A CUM LINE WITH A PARETO DIAGRAM
USED TO REPRESENT A QUALITY IMPROVEMENT.

and-effect diagram. Due to its visual effect, a diagram of this type looks like a fishbone, hence the name Fishbone Diagram, or Ishikawa Diagram after Professor Kaoru Ishikawa who invented it.

The steps in the construction of a cause-and-effect diagram are given in Figure 3.12 and are as follows:

- The problem to be analyzed is represented by a box with an arrow running into it from the left (step 1).

(a) Represent the problem (step 1)

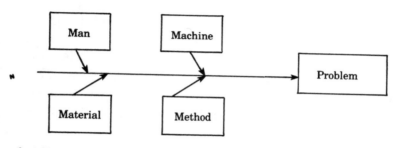

(b) Add the major causes (step 2)

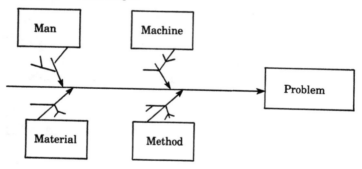

(c) Add the minor causes around the major causes (step 3)

FIGURE 3.12   STEPS IN THE CONSTRUCTION OF A
BASIC CAUSE-AND-EFFECT DIAGRAM.

- The circle members, through group techniques, identify major causes, which are connected to the main arrow by slanting arrows and are labeled (step 2).
- Minor causes are determined and connected

by arrows to the major causes and are labeled (step 3).

After the diagram is completed, the members vote on the causes they feel are most important, as in brainstorming. The important causes thus identified are further studied for problem resolution.

The construction of a cause-and-effect diagram is a dynamic process that requires a high level of member interaction. A sparse diagram reflects a shallow knowledge of the process. A bushy diagram reflects a quality session in which the circle leader did not effectively control the group discussion.

PROCESS CAUSE-AND-EFFECT

It is also useful to model a cause-and-effect diagram after the steps in a production process. This type of analysis is particularly useful for assembly line problems.

The steps in the construction of a process cause-and-effect diagram are given in Figure 3.13 and are as follows:

- The problem to be analyzed is represented by a box with an arrow running into it from the left (step 1).
- The steps in the production sequence are established by working forward, backward, or in both directions (step 2).
- Major and minor causes are determined and are connected by arrows to the boxes representing the production sequence (step 3).

(a) Represent the problem (step 1)

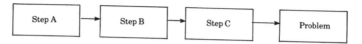

(b) Determine the steps in the process (step 2)

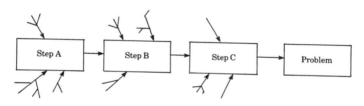

(c) Suggest the major and minor causes (step 3)

FIGURE 3.13   STEPS IN THE CONSTRUCTION OF A
PROCESS CAUSE-AND-EFFECT DIAGRAM.

In this method, the major and minor causes are identified by brainstorming and, as before, quality circle members vote on the most important items for further analysis.

This type of diagram is easy to make and understand because it closely models the real process. A minor disadvantage is that the same causes tend to appear as arrows attached to several steps in the sequence and the "bushiness" of the diagram tends to increase rapidly.

Applicatives

An *applicative* is the application of two or more data collection and analysis methods in succession to solve a quality circle problem. As an example of the concept, assume the existence of a complex manufacturing quality problem as suggested by Figures 3.3 and 3.6. A representative applicative for this problem is given as follows:

- The major quality problem is recognized. Major failures are listed.
- A check sheet is designed to collect the quality data.
- Production data is collected.
- A frequency or percentage histogram is constructed.
- From the histogram, a Pareto diagram is developed.
- The major problems are isolated.
- Process cause-and-effect diagrams are constructed through knowledge of the sequence of steps in the production procedure and the method of brainstorming.
- Circle members vote on the most important causes.
- Through small-group dynamics, including further use of brainstorming and possibly other methods, tentative resolutions for the various causes are identified.
- Recommendations are presented to management for approval.

This applicative is typical of the series of steps that would take place for a certain class of problems in a quality circle. Clearly, each problem is unique in some way or another so that a good grasp of the quality circle methods is important. Experience is useful for designing applicatives, but basic knowledge of the methods is absolutely necessary. Thus, quality circle training is an ongoing activity.

Summary

The most prudent approach to quality circle implementation is to initiate a pilot project and measure the results. If results are favorable, then the program can be extended into other areas. Otherwise, the program can be discontinued or started in another area. An even more important reason to measure results from quality circle activities is that when political winds change and new management is not convinced of the value of quality circles, effective measurement can support and justify the continuation of the program. At the quality level, measurement and analysis techniques can be used for the identification, analysis and solution of problems, and to support recommendations to management.

Measurements to support, justify and analyze the operations of a quality circle program can be grouped into three categories: quality indicators, cost analysis, and attitude indicators. All quality improvements can be translated into either cost reductions or productivity gains. One of the most powerful and easily understood methods of projecting production and cost data to estimate the payback or improved cash flow of a proposed scheme is the learning curve.

A quality circle program represents an ongoing activity where new problems are continually being identified, analyzed and resolved. It can also significantly improve employee motivation through participative management.

Brainstorming is a group technique for generating ideas and is used in quality circle activities for identifying problems, uncovering probable causes, and developing viable solutions.

In manufacturing and other forms of commerce, a large amount of data is collected to form the basis for decisions and actions. Reasons for collecting data can be grouped into a few categories:

- Understanding the situation
- Serving as a basis for cause-and-effect analysis
- Regulating the process
- Supporting quality control
- Performing financial analysis

Two aspects of data collection are of prime importance: recording and presentation. For quality circle activities, four frequently-used recording methods are the check list, the drawing, the check sheet, and the computer printout. The most commonly-used methods for presenting collected data are line graphs, histograms, pie charts, and control charts.

Data analysis techniques facilitate the process of identifying problems, causes and solutions and for presenting recommendations to management. Two basic methods of data analysis are used in quality circle work: Pareto diagrams and cause-and-effect diagrams. The latter are further classed as "basic cause-and-effect" and "process cause-and-effect."

A Pareto diagram is a means of establishing and visualizing a priority among problems or causes. The combination of a cumulative line with a Pareto diagram is ideal for management presentations. A basic cause-and-effect diagram takes the form of a fishbone with large and small arrows representing major and minor causes for problem resolution. A process cause-and-effect diagram is used to model a basic cause-and-effect diagram after the steps in a production process. Major and minor causes are then identified for subsequent resolution.

An applicative is the application of two or more data collection and analysis methods in succession to solve a quality circle problem. Experience is useful for designing applicatives, but a basic knowledge of the methods is necessary.

IV

STRATEGIC PLANNING FOR QUALITY CIRCLES

Introduction

Quality circles are unique in that they combine a participative management technique with a (historically) structured working environment. The technique is, of course, quality circles implemented as a small group activity, and the working environment is the classical production shop. The latter can encompass workers in manufacturing, banking, offices, and all of the service industries. In short, production workers characteristically perform structured tasks—such as an assembly worker, bank teller, or inventory clerk—as contrasted to knowledge workers—such as a manager, scientist, engineer, or analyst—who characteristically perform less structured tasks.

Since diverse groups in a business enterprise are impacted by a quality circle program and the implications can be far-reaching, planning is particularly significant.

This chapter covers the key areas of strategic planning for quality circles, selection of projects,

89

justification and acceptance. Collectively, the information presented here can be used as a guideline for the development of a strategic plan for a quality circle pilot project and subsequently an overall quality and functional plan.

Systems Approach to Planning

It is important to recognize that a variety of group plans effectively feed into the total business plan, as shown in Figure 4.1. Due to the enthusiasm commonly associated with quality circles, the claims for success can easily lead to overly optimistic expectations. It is particularly significant that the "quality" component of the plan be developed on a firm foundation.

The systems approach to planning is an attempt to put as much precision into the planning process as possible. The interrelationships among groups are a dynamic process that is continually being restructured as business conditions change. Therefore, management should ensure that the

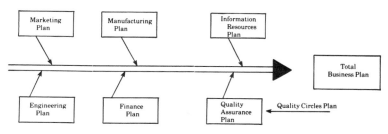

FIGURE 4.1 CONCEPTUAL "FISHBONE DIAGRAM" FOR THE TOTAL BUSINESS PLAN.

most appropriate concept is applied to the most pertinent problem at the most opportune time.

Systems analysis for the purpose of planning should proceed along at least four dimensions:

Congruence—the most appropriate concept is used at the proper time.

Integrity—the approach provides a complete solution to the problem as it is viewed by the organization.

Auditability—the process can be demonstrated to provide the results specified.

Controllability—the operation of the procedure can be effectively controlled by management.

In fact, a good strategic plan should specifically address each of the dimensions.

As a concept, quality circles are observable, capable of being described in terms of procedures, inputs, and outputs, and are amenable to experimental manipulation to verify (or support) their congruence, integrity, auditability and controllability.

Congruence is related to the logic of systems analysis and the degree to which it reflects the relative capital-labor ratio. The methods of quality circles may have too much overhead in terms of training, planning, involvement, and so forth to be applied to certain small-sized management or production problems. On the other hand, the concept may be too weak to even assist in solving large-scale interdepartmental and organizational problems. Quality circles should be used *only* when they are the most appropriate method.

Integrity is the degree to which a method or technique performs according to its specifications. In quality circles, there is an expected payoff in terms of improvements in costs, scheduling, quality, employee attitudes, and so forth. A quality circle is not a social gathering, and management should be able to predict—to some degree, anyway—what results can be expected of a quality circle program.

Auditability refers to the demonstrability of expected results through the observation of actual circle operations and the resulting management recommendations. In short, a quality circle program must produce results, and those results should end up on the proverbial bottom line. The results should be directly observable and measurable and not hidden in a myriad of production and/or operational facts and figures.

Controllability determines the extent to which management can control a quality circle program through directives, problem suggestions, the reward system, training, and actual management participation. Management should have direct or indirect control over the problems on which a quality circle works and should have a clear policy on how quality circle recommendations to management are handled. Clearly, management does not want to be faced with the situation of being coerced into accepting a recommended solution for fear of creating an adverse morale or attitude problem. There are two eventualities that management should absolutely avoid: (1) having the tail wag the dog, and (2) upsetting the apple cart through quality circles.

In short, a quality circle program should be describable and controllable, and the overall responses to business conditions should be predictable.

Strategy Concepts

A *strategy* is the means that management chooses to use an organization's resources to reach its objectives. Thus, a strategy is an implicit relationship involving the organization, its objectives, its resources, and its environment.

A *statement* of strategy is a mechanism for focusing the attention of management planners on a topic and serves as a communications medium for management review, approval and support. A statement of strategy includes, but is not limited to, the following topics:

- A comprehensive course of action
- Anticipated risks
- Organizational dependencies
- External business environment and conditions
- Required resources
- Financial requirements, conditions, and projections
- Viable alternatives

To make a strategy statement, a strategic planner must be involved with quality circle concepts, and should have knowledge of the organization's methods, history, planning and politics.

Another important consideration is that the

planner may not be a quality circle specialist, so some preparation may be required. The steps involved in developing a strategy are:

- Understand the scope and nature of the subject matter, as well as its organizational implications
- Describe the future environment
- Identify the objectives and the alternative possible strategies
- Set up criteria for the selection of an optimum strategy
- Select the preferred strategy
- Prepare the strategy statement
- Obtain strategy approval
- Take steps to incorporate a functional strategy for quality circles into the strategic and operating plans of the organization

It is important to recognize that a strategy is *not* a step-by-step plan for reaching a predetermined set of objectives, but rather is a metaplan. In this context, *metaplan* refers to the planning process about planning. Thus, a strategy paper should also delineate objectives and guidelines for the planning process itself, in addition to the preparation of operational plans and goals for the organization.

To sum up, therefore, the dimensions of a quality circle strategy are threefold:

- Directions and goals
- A guide for implementation
- A rationale for decision-making

It deals primarily with, "How do we get there from

here?" Effectively, a strategy provides relevant action for a future operational environment.

Strategy and Planning

The concept of a quality circle is not an end in itself. It is a method, albeit a general one, for organizational problems related to quality, performance, employee attitudes and motivation, scheduling, excessive costs, and so forth. The key question is not what should be done tomorrow, but rather, what should be done today to prepare for an uncertain future. A quality circle program may be implemented in a specific area, such as manufacturing or office automation, or it may involve the total organization. Nevertheless, an explicit decision is made to use quality circles. Organizations do not and should not employ the quality circle technique "on a whim" or because somebody likes the idea. The implementation of quality circles in your organization should be a direct response to an organizational need.

CONTENTS OF THE STRATEGY

A quality circle strategy gives three things:

- Where we are (*current position*)
- Where we are going (*goals*)
- How we get there (*direction*)

The *current position* is a specification of the equipment and supplies, tested applications, trained and knowledgeable people, and existing organizational problems that have a bearing on a quality circle plan. *Goals* include factors such as better customer service, increased sales volume with the same head count, reducing administrative expenses, job enhancement, the establishment of new markets, improved quality, reduced costs, and more timely and effective decision-making.

The *direction* is a major issue—in fact, it is the reason for a strategy in the first place. Direction requires policies and procedures in the following areas:

- Justification
- Implementation
- Employee acceptance
- Staffing and organization

These areas form the basis for a strategic plan that gives the stages of tactical (or functional) planning for the enterprise.

STRATEGIC PLAN

The strategic plan for a quality circle program covers three stages of work: preparatory, developing a tactical plan, and utilizing the tactical plan.

The *preparatory work* is crucial because it sets the stage for success or failure. The history of planning within an enterprise should first be consulted because a quality circle will eventually become part of a larger planning entity. A high-level management commitment—or sponsor—is needed to kickoff an effective project. Responsibility for a quality circle program and also for tactical planning should be assigned and a strategy group should be formed. Participation in any of the above activities need not be on a full-time basis; the key objective is to specify basic objectives and the output of the strategy sessions. Actually, an ad hoc task force to initiate a project, as outlined above, can be an effective course of action.

The sponsor is particularly significant because resources have to be obtained for a quality circle program and the needed policies must be set and enforced.

In *developing the plan,* assumptions must be made concerning the organizational structure, the staff, and the organizational implications. After gathering and analyzing information about the organization, a sequence of potential quality circle applications are selected. Objectives are required at this point; they must minimally include opportunities, goals that can be measured, time frames, and any problems that are anticipated. At this point, the strategic plan should be reviewed with local management and then presented to top management.

In *utilizing the plan,* approval is requested for initial activities that include pilot projects, research efforts, and associated development work. A means of using the plan is also needed, which includes people, procedures, and a user feedback channel. The plan should also include an action item to be updated in line with the planning policies of the enterprise.

GUIDELINES

In outlining a strategy and developing a plan for a quality circle program, a few pertinent guidelines are helpful for increasing the chance of project success. The most important consideration is to concentrate resources in time and place and to focus them on the stated objectives. Second, it is not prudent to allocate resources unless there is a better than average chance of success. There are simply too many intangibles in participative management to ensure immediate success, and employee acceptance can be problematical unless handled properly. It follows that proper consideration of employee reactions to a quality circle is an important aspect of strategic planning. Last, you shouldn't compete for the organization's resources unless the conditions are favorable to the capacities of your organizational unit, and you shouldn't try to obtain these resources unless they will contribute to your organizational unit's strategic objectives.

Justification

Enthusiasm over quality circles is contagious. The spirit of participative management, for example, is both exciting and interesting. It is unlikely that this enthusiasm will carry over to the executive suite, however, where seasoned executives will question the viability of the newly-discovered source of productivity. Therefore, justification will be required—regardless of the credibility of the sponsor.

DEFINITION

Justification is the information presented to a decision-maker to support an investment proposal. In general, there are two major reasons to provide justification:

1. To achieve agreement to put an investment proposal in an overall plan for the organization.
2. To obtain a commitment of resources for an implementation project.

METHODOLOGY

Traditional methods of justification include almost any form of inductive reasoning. Some of the more noteworthy are:

- Cost of participative management vs. the old method
- Improved customer service
- Gives a competitive advantage
- It is part of the cost of doing business
- It is our "image" to be at the leading edge
- Lower costs
- Improved quality
- Better employee attitudes and morale

With quality circles, a useful approach is to depict a labor cost curve with a flattened slope achieved by increasing the efficiency and effectiveness of the affected personnel. This is productivity.

PRODUCTIVITY

Productivity is a key benefit of the quality circle concept because it provides an increased quality and quantity of work, an increased span of control, more effective (i.e., more timely) work, and decreased turnover of key people. Thus, productivity can be more formally specified as the relationship between the output of a work environment to its input in labor and raw materials.

METHODS OF ANALYSIS

Two methods of delineating productivity are the payback method and the cash flow method.

The *payback method* reflects costs that are displaced because of the results of quality circle activities. Reduced material requirements in a processing operation, initiated as a quality circle recommendation to management, is an example of a case where costs are actually decreased.

With the *cash flow method,* costs are not reduced by the newer management philosophy, but the total output is greater for the same costs. A recommendation to reorganize the work area and promote team behavior is an example of how output could be increased without necessarily reducing costs.

In some cases, therefore, labor, equipment and facilities costs are displaced and *cost savings* result. Typical examples are floor space for files, travel costs, postage costs, forms and supplies costs, time savings, and reduced materials. In other cases, *cost avoidance* takes place because there is a decreased growth of staff, equipment and facilities to accompany an increased output level.

Implementation

The notion of *implementation* refers to a pilot project to establish the quality circle concept, and then an expansion both horizontally and vertically within the organization. Horizontal expansion refers to a proliferation of quality circles throughout the organization. Vertical expansion refers to an enhancement of the tasks that can be assigned to quality circles through training and increased experience in group problem-solving by the members.

THE PILOT PROJECT APPROACH

A pilot project is a forerunner of a larger project or application with the objective of building confidence in a new idea. It is a learning experience that demonstrates technical feasibility, costs, benefits and employee acceptance. Effectively, a "pilot" is a means of planning big and starting small.

A pilot project is an approach to experiential learning and to gauging resistance by employees, management and unions. Some approaches that have been taken are to give the quality circle program to some groups and not to others, or to implement the concept in all groups and then take it away from some of them. The objective in both cases is to measure productivity, have interviews, and give questionnaires to assess the success of the project.

In many cases—and particularly in the area of quality circle activities—management simply does not know to what extent employees can participate and how much they want to. A pilot project is a means of determining valuable input to the planning process without spending an excessive amount of money. It is also a means of finding mistakes and problems early and thereby minimizing exposure. If a pilot project flops, it is chalked up to experience. If a heavily committed project fails, it is blamed on more serious factors.

SELECTING A CLIMATE FOR SUCCESS

The best pilot project for quality circle activities is naturally one with a high probability of success. The object shop or department should contain problems to be solved, but not so many that the probability of success is low. The project should be assigned to a relatively small close-knit group with good internal communication (so they can aid one another) and an enthusiastic manager. Most importantly, a pilot project must not be placed in a pressure group that may not give a concept a fair evaluation.

The time duration for a pilot project must be long enough for the shop or department people to become accustomed to the methods, but short enough so the momentum and enthusiastic atmosphere does not subside. Most experts agree that two to six months is the optimum duration.

CHOOSING THE RIGHT SHOP OR DEPARTMENT

Since quality circle activities are dependent upon employee contributions, it is necessary to measure their reactions to the pilot project. Interviews and questionnaires are the best methods of assessment. If a person can achieve personal success through quality circle participation, then he will be the best source of support.

Employee Acceptance

A quality circle program is an agent of change, so the success of a project is largely dependent upon the reactions of employees and management to it. It is important that the people regard the implementation phase as, "This is *our* system." As a result, much of change management is dependent upon an acceptance strategy, resistance management, and proper education and training.

ACCEPTANCE STRATEGY

A successful acceptance strategy is anticipatory, so fears, resistance and expectations must be identified early in the implementation plan. The announcement of the plan should be made early in the change cycle, and significant policy questions have to be addressed. Making a general announcement of a quality circle program, however, and then limiting the initial implementation phase to a few departments can lead to negative results, since enthusiasm can quickly become dampened when expectations are not satisfied. As a result, careful attention should be given to the manner in which pilot projects and early implementation plans are introduced.

The "kickoff" announcement should in general be made to the affected departments by a high-level executive who describes the objectives, benefits to the individual and the organization, expectations, feedback mechanism, and user implementation schedule.

The acceptance strategy is a link between the strategic and tactical plans of an enterprise and covers personnel policies regarding participation, management support, training, rewards and recognition, management recommendations, and the support of labor groups.

THE MANAGEMENT OF RESISTANCE

Some of the factors that contribute to reduced resistance are also good management practices in general. A significant aspect to consider in this area is that the members of a quality circle team will probably not be experienced in group dynamics and will therefore be hesitant to offer views because of the possibility of being "shot down." Fear of reprisal for nonparticipation is also a latent fear and may foster a feeling of coercion in some people. Also, management's presentation of a group's recommendation can easily lead to "no recommendation" if the members fear the process. The biggest resistance by far can come from foremen and supervisors who feel threatened by the process of giving some of the action to employees. Especially cumbersome are foremen who run a "tight ship" and tend to interpret any suggestion as a crack in the wall of authority. This is one reason why it is a good idea to start with the foreman or supervisor as the circle leader. However, it may take considerable coaxing by the facilitator and departmental management to allow the leader's position to be turned over to a member.

EDUCATION AND TRAINING

The existence of training programs in modern organizations is presently taken for granted. It is supplied by practically all organizations in every sphere of activity.

An integral part of a quality circle program is the training of all members. Basic to planning, however, is the not-so-obvious fact that three types of learning actually take place. The most widely recognized form is the process of acquiring knowledge and understanding; this includes gaining ideas, principles, concepts and facts. Another type of learning is skill acquisition, which may include group participation in quality circle activities as well as work tasks. The last type of learning is the changing of attitudes, interests, and goals. Only the factual form of learning takes place in sessions held by the leader and facilitator. The second and third types of learning are restricted to participation and quality circle activities.

Fortunately, the learning curve comes into play for all three types of learning so that most participants can contribute substantially after a few training sessions and quality circle meetings.

Summary

Quality circles are unique in that they combine a participative management technique with a structured working environment. The technique is quality circles implemented as a small group activity, and the working environment is the classical production shop. The notion of a production shop can encompass workers in manufacturing, banking, offices, and all of the service industries.

A variety of group plans effectively feed into the total business plan. The systems approach to planning is an attempt to put as much precision into the planning process as possible. Management should ensure that the most appropriate concept is applied to the most pertinent problem at the most opportune time. The key dimensions of systems analysis for planning are:

- Congruence
- Integrity
- Auditability
- Controllability

A quality circle program should be describable and controllable, and the overall response to business conditions should be predictable.

A *strategy* is the means that management chooses to use an organization's resources to reach its objectives. It is an implicit relationship involving the organization, its objectives, its resources, and its environment. A statement of strategy is a mechanism for focusing the attention of management planners on a topic and serves as a communications medium for management review, approval and support. A strategy statement normally includes the following topics:

- Course of action
- Risks

- Dependencies
- Business environment and conditions
- Resources
- Financial facts
- Alternatives

A strategic planner must be involved with quality circle concepts.

The dimensions of a quality circle strategy are threefold:

- Directions and goals
- A guide for implementation
- A rationale for decision-making

The steps in the planning process are well-defined and easy to understand.

A quality circle program should be a direct response to an explicit organizational need. A quality circle strategy gives three things:

- The current position
- Goals
- Direction

While the current position and goals are necessary, the direction is a major issue because it serves to establish policies and procedures in the following areas: justification, implementation, employee acceptance, and staffing and organization.

The success of a strategic plan is dependent upon good preparatory work and a sponsor within the organization. Acceptance of a plan is dependent upon justification, which involves both agreement and a commitment of resources. Methods of measuring productivity include the payback method and the cash flow method.

The implementation of a strategic plan for quality circles normally involves a pilot project followed by horizontal and vertical expansion within the organization. Significant factors include choosing the right application and ensuring that there is a climate for success. Employee and management acceptance is directly related to resistance management and effective education and training.

Part Three:

ORGANIZA-
TIONAL
DYNAMICS

V

HUMAN RELATIONS

Introduction

The recognition and acceptance of quality circles is one of the most significant results to come out of the excellence movement. On the other hand, the notion that all an organization needs is a quality circle program and henceforth all problems will be solved is far from the truth.

The biggest problem is management itself. In fact, certain segments of the "frozen middle," as modern middle management is affectionately known, are emphatically against any organization, formal or informal, supposedly telling them what to do.

Most participants in a quality circle program have worked together prior to initiation of the circle. Quality circle participation, however, is so different that some participants may feel a bit disoriented. This is so within an authoritative organization. Some workers are simply not accustomed to having other participants listen to them and then, to top it off, having their opinions and ideas valued to a significant degree.

Recognizing that potential problems exist with management styles and group dynamics, this chapter surveys the current thinking in these areas.

Management Styles

It appears to be self-evident that management style determines to a large extent how a person views participative management. For example, one executive could view a recommendation for a quality circle as a definite threat, while another might view it as an opportunity. Four important topics are covered here: information space, decision processes, cognitive style, and the management environment.

INFORMATION SPACE

In management, administration, various work environments, and in personal life, persons respond to their own information spaces in a variety of ways. In this context, a person's *information space* refers to the informational environment in which he or she ordinarily operates, and usually consists of what a person knows in relation to what other people know.

This personal information space can be conceptualized through the use of a Johari window, created to model interpersonal communications. As shown in Figure 5.1, a Johari window is comprised of two axes and four quadrants. It con-

	INFORMATION KNOWN TO SELF	INFORMATION UNKNOWN TO SELF
INFORMATION KNOWN TO OTHERS	Open Area 1	Blind Area 2
INFORMATION UNKNOWN TO OTHERS	Hidden Area 3	Unknown Area 4

FIGURE 5.1 JOHARI WINDOW. (THE NAME IS DERIVED AS A COMBINATION OF JOE AND HARRY AFTER ITS ORIGINATORS: JOSEPH LUFT AND HARRY INGHAM.)

cerns behavior, feelings, and motivation known to a person's self and to others. Quadrant 1 denotes information known to the self and others and is called the *open area*. A large first quadrant represents good interpersonal relations, and working with others is thereby facilitated. A person with a large first quadrant has good contact with his or her environment, and he or she and others are aware of abilities and needs.

Quadrant 2 is known as the *blind area* and represents information known to others but not to one's self. This quadrant reflects a degree of vulnerability at the interpersonal level. For example, an arrogant person may misinterpret his or her own behavior as self-assertiveness and not recognize the extent to which others may mistrust him or her.

Quadrant 3 signifies information known to

one's self and not to others and is known as the *hidden area*. This may be largely governed by social custom or business etiquette and normally involves personal motivations, aspirations and feelings. Information in this area is concealed from others; disclosure about one's self reduces the hidden area and increases the open area. Since a person is effectively in charge of self-disclosure, a balance of spontaneity and discretion effectively determines the efficiency of this quadrant.

Finally, the fourth quadrant—the *known area*—refers to information not known to the self and to others. This area can represent untapped resources. Experiences and events associated with the fourth quadrant can lead to new opportunities that a person and others did not know were available. For example, assuming leadership in a small group situation can reveal behavior that increases the size of the open area.

The Johari window can reflect various forms of communication. As represented in Figure 5.2a,

GIVING FEEDBACK

Open Area 1	Blind Area 2
Hidden Area 3	Unknown Area 4

(a)

RECEIVING FEEDBACK

Open Area 1	Blind Area 2
Hidden Area 3	Unknown Area 4

(b)

FIGURE 5.2   THE EFFECT OF FEEDBACK.

giving feedback reduces the size of the hidden area and increases the size of the open area. Receiving feedback reduces the size of the blind area and increases the size of the open area.

The information space is an important consideration in how management relates to a quality circle and also within the group dynamics of the circle itself.

DECISION PROCESSES

Decision processes can be viewed from two perspectives: according to the information required and by the steps involved in reaching a solution. Both perspectives are relevant to management and circle activities. The former perspective is covered here and the latter is covered within the scope of quality circles.

Information is distilled through analysis techniques that include composition, selection, summarization, consolidation and transformation. The process is analogous to water being fed from tributaries into a river. Before long, the water from the various sources is all mixed up. Distilled information is combined with experience, intelligence and intuition on the part of the decision-maker in the decision process. The output is the resulting action. Experience, intelligence and intuition constitute *judgment.*

Decisions that involve only information are known as *structured decisions.* This type of decision represents "economic man" and applies to inventory management, manufacturing control, and so forth. Decisions involving the information dimension and managerial judgment are called *semistructured decisions.* Decisions in this category include budgeting, forecasting, tactical planning, and some forms of financial analysis.

Decisions involving judgment alone are known as *unstructured decisions* and are customarily associated with strategic and long-range planning.

Unstructured decisions depending completely on managerial judgment are heavily related to a manager's cognitive style.

COGNITIVE STYLE

The thinking style of executives, managers, administrators and workers determines how they organize information to achieve the awareness required for effective group participation and decision-making. The *scope* of a decision situation is determined by how a person reads the environment. The *extent* of a person's activities is governed by an assessment of his or her perceived job role.

Diversity of scope and extent yields two personal styles: the systematic person and the intuitive person. A *systematic person* uses "hard" information and an *intuitive person* uses "soft" information. The choice of style should depend on the decision situation and include a bit of both processes.

Personal style has been identified with the side of the brain that is predominantly used in various forms of behavior. Research has shown that, for most people, the left hemisphere of the brain performs logical processes that have a linear order, such as reading, problem-solving, and planning. The right hemisphere of the brain operates in a parallel fashion on holistic and relational processes. Visual image processes and intuitive judgment are right-side functions. Well-developed right-hemisphere functions enable an executive, for example, to deal effectively with "soft" speculative inputs. To some extent, this research has explained the propensity of most executives to prefer the verbal mode of communication. Speech is linear, but the total process allows managers to read facial expressions, gestures, and various voice forms. Most activities involve both sides of the brain, but some individuals prefer to use their dominant side.

Of the various tasks associated with decision-making, two are specifically identified with cognitive style and split-brain functioning: diagnosis of a decision situation and design of a viable solution.

Diagnosis of a decision situation is the perceptual process of information gathering in either of two modes: the perceptive mode or the receptive mode. A *perceptive modality* involves analyzing the relationships among data groups, filtering data, and synthesizing definitive information from available data. A *receptive modality* involves focusing on details and stresses the completeness, consistency and integrity of data. The disadvantages of both modalities are obvious. With perception, important details can be overlooked. With reception, the gestalt may not be recognized. Participative management and consensus decision-making ostensibly combine the advantages of the perceptive and receptive modalities while minimizing the disadvantages.

The design of a viable solution refers to the process of problem-solving. A *systematic modality* involves the structuring of a decision problem into well-defined subproblems, each with a known feasible solution. Information is utilized as it fits the solution through relevant cognitive models. Thus, *the method is the solution.* In an *interactive modality,* an incremental form of problem-solving is used wherein an individual makes an incremental move in a viable direction without assessing the total situation due to economic, political, social, or physical reasons.

MANAGEMENT ENVIRONMENT

The leadership style evidenced by most executives, managers, and administrators can be placed into four well-known categories or combinations of them: automatic, bureaucratic, democratic, and laissez-faire. The leadership style of management, per se, is not significant with regard to the acceptance of quality circles. It is the problem-solving modality (i.e., systematic or intuitive) and mode of information gathering (i.e., perceptive or receptive), together with leadership style that really count.

From a quality circle viewpoint, therefore, the problems to be solved and the manner in which solutions are presented to management should be based on the managerial environment.

Individuals and the Organization

The modern work environment has come a long way since the days of Frederick Taylor, who proposed in the 1800s that performance was directly related to monetary reward; the greater the reward, the greater the productivity. Today, the worker is known to be motivated by sex, benefits, money, responsibility, ego, recognition, a sense of accomplishment, personal needs satisfaction, and personal development. Quality circles are based on an employee's need to participate in the worker environment in line with these motivational factors. Moreover, it is fully recognized that persons participate for different reasons. Several theories of motivation exist, and it may be wise to use them as a basis for group dynamics.

One of the pioneers of motivation theory was Maslow, who hypothesized that people are motivated by a hierarchy of needs. Maslow identified five categories (reading from top to bottom): self-actualization, ego, social, security, and physical. The basis of Maslow's theory is that people are motivated to satisfy the lower needs first (i.e., physical, then security, and so forth). Higher-level needs only become motivating factors when low-level needs are satisfied. Moreover, once a need is satisfied, it no longer becomes a motivator.

McClelland took an orthogonal view to the processes of motivation. He maintained that a person's needs are based on personal experiences that cause the individual to be motivated by achievement, power, or affiliation. Persons oriented toward achievement look for challenge, recognition, and an assurance of how well he or she is doing. Persons oriented toward power seek control and influence and manifest this need through a person or social process. Persons seeking personal power exhibit their leadership by developing subordinates without dominating them. Last, persons oriented toward affiliation look for relationships by supporting others and maintaining equilibrium.

The most widely quoted behaviorist is probably McGregor, who espoused Theories X and Y. McGregor was concerned with management style, which effectively determines how people are motivated. The assumption with Theory X management style is that people inherently dislike work and have little ambition. They must be threatened by management to provide suitable performance. McGregor claimed that Theory X management is ineffective (based on motivation theories). Moreover, the Theory X assessment of workers simply isn't true in the modern world. He proposed a management style based on assumptions—known as Theory Y—wherein people seek rewards, achievement, the processes of work, and the challenge of working toward organizational goals. In addition, a coercive style of management has a negative effect on motivation. McGregor's work has formed the basis for much of management thinking in the past thirty years.

Herzberg proposed a two-factor theory of motivation. "Motivator" factors cause a person to be satisfied with his or her job; "hygiene" factors, if absent, cause a person to be dissatisfied. The *motivator factors,* involving job content, are achievement, recognition, the work process, responsibility, and advancement. The *hygiene factors,* involving job context, are company policy and administration, supervision, interpersonal relations with peers, interpersonal relations with subordinates, salary, job security, personal life, work conditions and status. Thus, to properly motivate employees, an organization must maintain hygiene factors and enhance motivator factors.

Motivation theories are pretty much known by all managers and most employees. They are, in fact, what participants seek in quality circle activities, which by definition are voluntary. When a circle stops being a motivating factor, then it logically ceases to exist.

Group Dynamics

Most persons are members of a group: the tennis team or the jogging club, a religious group or the PTA. In spite of this, group activities are fraught with problems. Often, group problems are the result of too many leaders or no leader, no ground rules, straying from the task, or a resistance to the team concept. Accordingly, it is important to consider what makes a group effective and how it should conduct business.

THE EFFECTIVE GROUP

There are a lot of reasons why groups stay together and achieve results—a particular problem, the participants have special needs, or extraordinary conditions existing at the time the group became operational. Johnson and Johnson (1982) describe nine requirements for effective groups that exist independently of special considerations: (1) goals are understood and evoke commitment; (2) members communicate accurately and clearly; (3) members share participation and leadership; (4) decision-making tools are appropriate to the situation; (5) members share power and influence; (6) conflicts are encouraged and well-managed; (7) problem-solving skills are developed; (8) group cohesion is high; and (9) the interpersonal effectiveness of members is high.

In short, groups work because the members are motivated to work together. In a quality circle context, cooperation can be achieved through member, leader, and facilitator training, and through hands-on experience in group participation.

GROUP DEVELOPMENT

A quality circle is formed to solve a class of problems. Except in very democratic organizations, this is unusual in the workplace. The facilitator must form the group and nurture it until it achieves sufficient independence to focus on a task. The steps through which group development must go are forming, storming, norming, and performing (see Tuckman, 1965).

In the *forming stage,* there is a tentativeness among members in expressing their opinion and a noticeable dependence on the leader or facilitator to "carry the ball." The members are trying to determine their place in the group and to identify the tasks they should perform. Either formally or informally, members attempt to establish procedures for the operation of the group.

In the *storming stage,* there is a normal conflict among members and between members and the leader. The authority of the leader is questioned as are the procedures established in the forming phase. There is some resistance to attempting and even accomplishing the task. In some cases, there is an innate fear of failure. The storming stage is a natural successor to the forming stage and a predecessor to the norming stage.

In the *norming stage,* the members begin to focus on a problem and norms of behavior are accepted. Group cohesion develops and members begin to trust each other. During this phase, the leader is sensitive to procedural issues that could disrupt efficient and effective operation of the group.

In the *performing stage,* a sense of group identity develops. Members freely ask for advice and give assistance. The group works toward a goal and strong ties are developed between members. The leader can sustain the group and members have a sense of pride in their achievements.

Clearly, the development of a group is dependent upon the behavior of its members. This fact is so critical for quality circle activities that a Quality Circle Code of Conduct was given as Table 2.8 in Chapter II.

Effective group behavior is dependent upon a clearly identified task. When a goal ceases to exist, group behavior deteriorates. Thus, a *terminat-*

ing stage is recognized as a necessary eventuality. Organizations handle this phase differently.

COOPERATIVE BEHAVIOR

Another subject that effectively governs the activity of a group is the roles members choose to assume. Beene and Sheats (1948) identify twelve task roles: initiator, information seeker, opinion seeker, information giver, opinion giver, elaborator, coordinator, orienter, evaluator, energizer, procedure technician, and recorder. The *initiator* proposes new ideas, tasks or goals, and suggests procedures for solving a problem or organizing group activity. The *information seeker* asks for relevant facts on a problem being discussed or on ideas being evaluated. The *opinion seeker* seeks clarification of issues related to a problem, idea or suggestion. The *information giver* provides pertinent information about a current topic. The *opinion giver* offers an opinion on ideas or suggestions, often based on personal values rather than facts. The *elaborator* gives examples relevant to a topic. The *coordinator* describes relationships between ideas or suggestions and identifies key points and possible alternatives. The *orienter* discusses the direction of the group relative to stated tasks or goals. The *evaluator* goes deeply into the logic behind alternatives and the pertinence of ideas and suggestions. The *energizer* tries to keep the group moving toward a goal. The *procedure technician* keeps group activities going by not allowing it to become distracted by procedural details. Lastly, the *recorder* functions as a group memory.

Clearly, not all task roles are positive; some are negative. The role assumed by a member depends somewhat on that person's motivational factors and the problem to be solved. The process by which a member assumes a role is based on the reward system. Positive roles are reinforced and emulated. Negative roles are discouraged by a similar process. After good quality circle member training programs, members can often identify the roles that they and co-members play by name.

On the other hand, a small collection of roles is necessary for the effective functioning of a group. Initially, the leader or facilitator must assume these roles, but later, through the reward/reinforcement system mentioned previously, members gradually pick them up. Group maintenance roles include: the encourager, harmonizer, compromiser, gatekeeper, standard setter, observer/commentator, and the follower. The *encourager* offers praise and accepts the ideas and suggestions of others. The *harmonizer* provides a relief from tension through humor and by giving timely feedback. The *compromiser* smooths things over when a group member's ideas are challenged. The *gatekeeper* is concerned with communication and suggests procedures for encouraging participation. The *standard setter* is concerned with the proper level of activity for the group to maintain and the quality of problem-solving. The *observer/commentator* helps the group evaluate its own procedures and functioning. Last, the *follower* accepts the ideas and suggestions of others—a role all members must assume at one time or another. The set of roles that participants choose to assume and those necessary for the effective functioning of a group are not disjoint. Moreover, positive roles are not necessary—perhaps only desirable from the viewpoint of good interpersonal relations.

There are also individual roles occasionally played by group members. These eight individual roles, not necessarily negative, are: the aggressor, blocker, recognition seeker, confessor, playboy, dominator, help seeker, and the special interest pleader. Probably every member at one time or another assumes an individual role, but preferably not all of the time. Individual roles are interesting once recognized and understood. After all, a quality circle would not be a practical working group without a playboy or confessor.

CONFLICT MANAGEMENT

It is inevitable that conflicts arise in task-oriented group processes, and this may be a negative feature for higher management prepared to support a quality circle program. The psychological climate is observable, however, and conflicts are predictable. Also, the effect of conflicts can be minimized by good management during meetings.

A good meeting should be orchestrated before, during, and after. Like music, the result will have lasting value. The *before* planning should emphasize two activities: (1) plan the topic, goals, attendance, and time, and (2) develop and distribute an agenda. The *during* activities should include: (1) review minutes, and (2) follow the prepared agenda. The *after* activities should encompass: (1)

set agenda for the next meeting, (2) check for satisfaction among members, and (3) delineate follow-up actions. Good meeting management will not eliminate conflicts, but a lack of planning will certainly cause them.

The psychological climate can be observed because the atmosphere and members' reactions to it are revealed by their behavior. From the ambiance of the group situation, the feelings of the members can be determined. Is there a sense of warmth, boredom, defensiveness, anger, frustration, or cooperation? Members may deliberately provoke others. There may be negative attitudes toward the ongoing task. It is possible that the expression of feelings and opinions is being thwarted. There may be cliques or subgroups. Some members may appear to be outside of the group.

The psychological climate can be determined by the roles members adopt and how behavior deviates from the norms established in earlier sessions. It is important to recognize what behaviors are and are not accepted and how individual members deal with violations of the norms. The circle leader must take over during periods of conflict by recognizing a potential problem and interjecting key remarks, such as, "Tell me what you think," "How do you feel about it?" "Give me your suggestions." The key point is that *the leader should listen, and members will emulate his or her response to the conflict situation.* Conflicts occur because of differences, and it is necessary for the leader to spot these differences. Differences commonly occur over the following items: facts, objectives, procedures, policy, ethics, and perceptions. A member may assume a role—such as the procedure technician—and then be at odds with fellow members over the manner in which the session is being run. The leader must resolve situations such as this by sharing items of agreement and summarizing points of disagreement. In many cases, it is only necessary to identify a disagreement and members will respond in a positive manner. Alternatives should always be listed because it provides a mechanism for compromise. Last, personal relationships should be maintained. The worst thing to happen in a group situation is to have members refuse to talk to or listen to another member.

Conflicts may arise over improper feedback, since communication problems seem to be at the heart of poor interpersonal relations. Some guidelines for giving feedback are:

1. The feedback should be specific and timely.
2. The feedback should relate to specific behavior.
3. Feedback should be constrained to items or behavior that can be changed.
4. Behavior should not be interpreted or evaluated—only stated as events.
5. Persons should not be evaluated—only ideas.
6. Feedback should be given only to assist or to encourage a member; positive feedback should be reinforced.

CONSENSUS

Consensus is defined as a collective opinion of a group achieved through a process of open communication in which all members participate. It is normally accepted by participants after they have had the opportunity to influence the decision, even though their views may be in the minority.

The other forms of decision-making that differ from consensus are:(1) decision by authority without discussion, (2) decision by expert, (3) decision by authority after discussion, (4) minority rule, (5) majority rule, and (6) averaging opinions. It is not uncommon in modern organizations to have opinions voiced by a group and a decision made by authority, but this is not the way in quality circle activities.

Several useful guidelines are available to participants in consensus decision-making. It is important to *state your position*. Others may adopt your ideas because they are sound. If they are not, stating them will help you realize why they are not particularly appropriate. If it is an outright difference of value, then you have done all you can.

Explore conflicts and expect differences of opinion. As in conflict management, identify items of disagreement and center discussions around them. Try to really understand other points of view. Listen to what people say—not how they say it.

Avoid techniques that easily reduce conflict. Majority vote, averaging, and bargaining should be applied only when necessary. There are no automatic winners or losers. If a member happens to be outvoted, there is no good reason to allow him or her to "win" on another issue.

It is sometimes necessary to take a strong position on an issue, but normally, a careful explanation of one's opinion is all that is necessary.

VI

GROUP DECISION-MAKING

Introduction

The context of a group decision is characterized by a focus, a set of factors, and a set of alternatives. The *focus* is the problem about which the decision has to be made, the *factors* are the criteria on the basis of which a choice will be made, and the *alternatives* are the possible choices. When choosing a new sports car, for example, the factors could be price, comfort, performance, and maintenance. Accordingly, the alternatives could be Corvette, Jaguar, and Porsche.

The factors need not reflect all of the attributes that the alternatives possess—only those that the group decision-makers collectively agree are relevant to their problem. Similarly, the alternatives may be only a subset of all possible choices open to the group. The process may be a subjective one, but that is nevertheless characteristic of decision processes in particular and human affairs in general.

In a group situation, the delineation of factors

131

and alternatives could be hard work but is relatively straightforward. Assigning priorities to the factors, on the other hand, could be very cumbersome unless a methodology is employed. A simple ranking system could be used, but it would tend to obscure needed detail. Ranking only reflects relative positions, whereas a numerical scale reflects a mass function.

For example, assume factor sets F and G. Factor set F has priorities and weights of $f_1 = 0.9$, $f_2 = 0.8$, $f_3 = 0.2$, and factor set G has priorities and weights of $g_1 = 0.9$, $g_2 = 0.2$, $g_3 = 0.1$. Clearly, f_2 and g_2 have the same rank but markedly different priorities.

A reasonably new method has been described by Saaty (1982) in his book entitled *Decision Making for Leaders*. It serves as the basis for this chapter, which covers the basic ideas and a few examples. More detailed information on the consistency of decisions and other mathematical topics can be obtained from the book itself. However, the subject matter covered here is sufficiently self-contained to be used in an ordinary decision-making situation.

Analytical Hierarchy Process

The *analytical hierarchy process* is a means of structuring a decision problem as a hierarchy, establishing priorities, and then combining the information to facilitate decision-making. The basis of the method is a hierarchy diagram that depicts the elements of the decision process.

HIERARCHIES

A decision hierarchy reflects the environment surrounding a problem and gives the factors and alternatives that contribute to a solution. The hierarchy is represented as a diagram.

At the topmost level of the diagram, which is structured as a tree, is the objective of the decision known as the *focus*. Figure 6.1 depicts the structure of a decision hierarchy. In the second level, factors are given and linked to the focus.

At the lowest level in the diagram is the set of alternatives. For each factor (i.e., each attribute), the complete set of alternatives is represented. This is important because each alternative should possess each of the attributes, or vice versa, as shown in the hierarchical diagram. Figure 6.2 gives an example of a hierarchical diagram that represents the sports car selection process, introduced earlier.

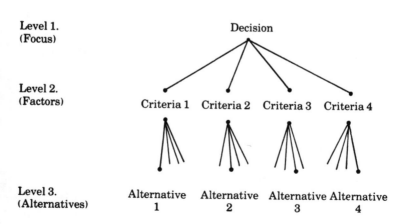

FIGURE 6.1   STRUCTURE OF A DECISION HIERARCHY.

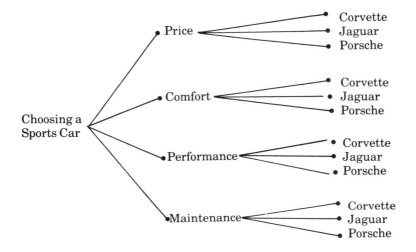

FIGURE 6.2   HIERARCHICAL DIAGRAM FOR THE
HYPOTHETICAL SPORTS CAR SELECTION PROCESS.

The basic idea of the diagram is to depict the various factors that influence the outcome of a decision. In a traditional decision support system (DSS) environment, factors can have subfactors, and so forth. In a group situation, there is a practical limit to the level of detail with which several people can collectively work. Accordingly, only the focus, factors and alternatives are covered here.

COMPARISONS

To establish a priority among the factors, it is necessary to compute the significance of each element on the next higher level. For example, in choosing a sports car, the relative importance of price, comfort, performance, and maintenance must be assessed to instantiate the basic criteria for the decision. Similarly, the comparative advantage of each model for each factor must be ascertained to relate the decision criteria to the decision environment.

Therefore, the criteria at each level must be compared on a pairwise basis. For this purpose, a preference matrix is used. Figure 6.3 gives an example.

In a preference matrix, the factors are listed at the column to the left and on the row at the top. The element on the left is compared with the corresponding element on the top. For example, performance (X) is compared with comfort (C) giving a value of 4. The meaning of the comparison should be somewhat as follows: "How much more important is the first element compared with the second element for this decision?" In this case, performance has a pairwise comparison value of 5 compared with comfort. Any viable scale could be used, such as, "Performance is four times more important than comfort."

Saaty (1982, p. 78) has proposed the compari-

	P	**C**	**X**	**M**
Price (P)	1	2	1/3	1/5
Comfort (C)	1/2	1	1/4	1/7
Performance (X)	3	7	2	1
Maintenance (M)	5	7	2	1

FIGURE 6.3   PREFERENCE MATRIX FOR THE DECISION
FACTORS FOR THE SPORTS CAR EXAMPLE.

TABLE 6.1   PAIRWISE COMPARISON SCALE.

Importance	Definition
1	Equal
3	Weak preference
5	Strong preference
7	Demonstrated importance
9	Absolute importance

Values 2, 4, 6, and 8 represent intermediate values

son scale summarized in Table 6.1. In the previous example, performance is strongly preferred to comfort, and maintenance is weakly preferred to performance with a value of 2. The comparisons may also reflect an opinion or preference on the importance of numeric values, such as price. The first item in a comparison is always the element in the left-hand column (such as price) and the second element is the element in the row across the top (such as maintenance). This comparison, judging from Figure 6.3, has a value of 1/5, which is the reciprocal of the comparison of maintenance with price.

It is always best to fill in the preferred entries. The transposed entries can then be entered by taking the reciprocal.

PRIORITIES

The priorities are computed in three steps. First, the entries in each column are added, as demonstrated in Figure 6.4. Second, the entries in each column are divided by its column total. This is

	P	**C**	**X**	**M**
Price (P)	1	2	1/3	1/5
Comfort (C)	1/2	1	1/4	1/7
Performance (X)	3	4	1	1/2
Maintenance (M)	5	7	2	1
Column Totals	9.5	14	3.58	1.84

FIGURE 6.4 ADDING THE ENTRIES IN EACH COLUMN OF
A PREFERENCE MATRIX.

called "normalization," yielding a *normalized preference matrix* (see Figure 6.5). Last, the values in each row are averaged by adding each row and dividing by the number of entries. This last operation yields the *priorities,* as demonstrated in Figure 6.6.

In this example, maintenance has the highest relative priority with .53 and comfort has the lowest with .07.

COMPUTING PRIORITIES FOR THE ALTERNATIVES

Once the priority vector for the factors has been computed, the next step in the analytical hierar-

	P	**C**	**X**	**M**
Price (P)	.11	.14	.09	.11
Comfort (C)	.05	.07	.07	.08
Performance (X)	.32	.29	.28	.27
Maintenance (M)	.53	.50	.56	.54

FIGURE 6.5 NORMALIZED PREFERENCE MATRIX.

Factor	Computation	Priority
Price (P)	(.11 + .14 + .09 + .11)/3	.11
Comfort (C)	(.05 + .07 + .07 + .08)/3	.07
Performance (X)	(.32 + .29 + .28 + .27)/3	.29
Maintenance (M)	(.53 + .50 + .56 + .54)/3	.53

FIGURE 6.6   PRIORITIES.

chy process is to compute a priority vector for the alternatives for each factor. For example, Figure 6.7 gives a preference matrix for the factor *price* for the three alternatives Corvette (C), Jaguar (J), and Porsche (P).

Accordingly, the normalized preference matrix and the vector of priorities is computed for each factor (price, comfort, performance, and maintenance) with respect to each of the alternatives. These computations are given in Figure 6.8. It is obvious from the matrices that a pairwise comparison, according to the pairwise comparison scale (Table 6.1), is required between the alternatives for each factor. Thus, the result is a priority vector of the alternatives for each factor. In the ex-

Price	C	J	P
Corvette (C)	1	3	5
Jaguar (J)	1/3	1	2
Porsche (P)	1/5	1/2	1

FIGURE 6.7   PREFERENCE MATRIX FOR THE FACTOR *PRICE* WITH RESPECT TO THE ALTERNATIVES.

PRICE	C	J	P	C	J	P	PRICE
		Preference Matrix			Normalized Matrix		Vector of Priorities
Corvette (C)	1	3	5	.65	.67	.63	.65
Jaguar (J)	1/3	1	2	.22	.22	.25	.23
Porsche (P)	1/5	1/2	1	.13	.11	.13	.12
Column Total	1.53	4.5	8				

COMFORT	C	J	P	C	J	P	COMFORT
Corvette (C)	1	1/3	2	.22	.22	.22	.22
Jaguar (J)	3	1	6	.67	.67	.67	.67
Porsche (P)	1/2	1/6	1	.11	.11	.11	.11
Column Total	4.5	1.50	9				

PERFORMANCE	C	J	P	C	J	P	PERFORMANCE
Corvette (C)	1	5	1/3	.24	.38	.22	.28
Jaguar (J)	1/5	1	1/7	.05	.08	.20	.08
Porsche (P)	3	7	1	.71	.54	.68	.64
Column Total	4.2	13	1.47				

MAINTENANCE	C	J	P	C	J	P	MAINTENANCE
Corvette (C)	1	5	3	.65	.63	.67	.65
Jaguar (J)	1/5	1	1/2	.13	.13	.11	.12
Porsche (P)	1/3	2	1	.22	.25	.22	.23
Column Total	1.53	8	4.5				

FIGURE 6.8 PREFERRED AND NORMALIZED PREFERENCE MATRICES AND THE PRIORITY VECTORS FOR THE FACTORS WITH RESPECT TO THE ALTERNATIVES IN THE SPORTS CAR PROBLEM.

ample, the priority vector for the factor *performance* is:

Alternative	**Priority**
Corvette	.28
Jaguar	.08
Porsche	.64

	Price (.11)	Comfort (.07)	Performance (.29)	Maintenance (.53)	Decision Priorities
Corvette (C)	.64 (.11) +	.22 (.07) +	.28 (.29) +	.65 (.53)	.51
Jaguar (J)	.23 (.11) +	.67 (.07) +	.08 (.29) +	.12 (.53)	.16
Porsche (P)	.12 (.11) +	.11 (.07) +	.64 (.29) +	.23 (.53)	.33

FIGURE 6.9   TAKING THE DECISION. (THE ALTERNATIVE PRIORITY FOR EACH OF THE FACTORS IS WEIGHTED BY THE PRIORITY OF THE CORRESPONDING FACTOR.)

Thus far, the analytical hierarchy process reflects good common sense. The factors (price, comfort, performance, and maintenance) have a priority, and there is also a priority of alternatives (Corvette, Jaguar, and Porsche) for each factor reflecting the degree to which the criterion is satisfied by the various alternatives.

TAKING THE DECISION

The priority sets provide a basis for "taking the decision." As shown in Figure 6.9, the priority vector for the factors is weighted by the priority of the corresponding criterion. Saaty calls this synthesis process *hierarchical composition*.

The result is a composite picture of the *decision priorities* for the various alternatives. For this example, the composite priority vector is:

Alternative	Decision Priority
Corvette	.51
Jaguar	.16
Porsche	.33

In this example, the availability of good maintenance and the price swing the decision. (In each of the other "home" countries, the decision priorities would probably be different.)

It is important to recognize that the pairwise comparison scale permits subjective elements to be entered into the decision process.

Operational Considerations

A few additional subjects should be discussed before the analytical hierarchy process can be used in a group decision-making situation.

HANDLING SUBFACTORS

An important technique concerns handling subfactors without adding a level to the hierarchical structure diagram. The concept will be presented as an adjunct to the preceding example.

Whereas the factors of price, comfort and maintenance may be single-dimensional criteria, the factor of performance is certainly not. In fact, most people would say that sports car performance has at least three important components: handling, acceleration, and top speed. Assume this is the case. Accordingly, a complete hierarchical composition of priorities for the factor *performance* is given in Figures 6.10 through 6.12. The resulting priority vector for *performance* is given as follows:

Alternative	Priority Vector
Corvette	.38
Jaguar	.08
Porsche	.55

PERFORMANCE	Preference Matrix			Normalized Matrix			Priority Vector PERFORMANCE
	H	A	T	H	A	T	
Handling (H)	1	3	5	.65	.67	.63	.65
Acceleration(A)	1/3	1	2	.22	.22	.25	.23
Top Speed (T)	1/5	1/2	1	.13	.11	.13	.12
Column Total	1.53	4.5	8				

FIGURE 6.10   ANALYSIS OF SUBFACTORS FOR THE FACTOR *PERFORMANCE.*

HANDLING	C	J	P	C	J	P	HANDLING
Corvette (C)	1	5	1/3	.24	.38	.22	.28
Jaguar (J)	1/5	1	1/7	.05	.08	.10	.08
Porsche (P)	3	7	1	.71	.54	.68	.64
Column Total	4.2	13	1.47				

ACCELERATION	C	J	P	C	J	P	ACCELERATION
Corvette (C)	1	8	5	.75	.53	.81	.70
Jaguar (J)	1/8	1	1/6	.10	.07	.03	.07
Porsche (P)	1/5	6	1	.15	.40	.16	.24
Column Total	1.33	15	6.17				

TOP SPEED	C	J	P	C	J	P	TOP SPEED
Corvette (C)	1	5	1/3	.24	.38	.22	.28
Jaguar (J)	1/5	1	1/7	.05	.08	.10	.08
Porsche (P)	3	7	1	.71	.54	.68	.64
Column Total	4.2	13	1.47				

(Note: Priority totals may not equal 1 due to rounding.)

FIGURE 6.11   COMPOSITE PRIORITIES FOR THE SUBFACTORS OF *PERFORMANCE.*

PERFORMANCE	Han-dling (.65)	Acceler-ation (.23)	Top Speed (.12)	Decision Priorities
Corvette (C)	.28 (.65) +	.70 (.23) +	.28 (.12)	.38
Jaguar (J)	.08 (.65) +	.07 (.23) +	.08 (.12)	.08
Porsche (P)	.64 (.65) +	.24 (.23) +	.64 (.12)	.55

FIGURE 6.12 HIERARCHICAL COMPOSITION FOR THE SUBFACTORS OF *PERFORMANCE*.

This agrees remarkably well with the priorities obtained through pairwise comparisons. In a real-life application, the result from a "subfactor analysis" could be used in lieu of a pairwise comparison of alternatives for that factor.

CONSISTENCY

An item that must be kept in mind when using the analytical hierarchy process is that the pairwise comparisons should be consistent. If, for example, A is preferred to B, and B is preferred to C, then it is inconsistent for C to be preferred to A. Careful attention should be given to consistency.

Advanced mathematical techniques are available for measuring consistency, but they are beyond the scope of this book. In general, however, consistency will not be a problem if thought is given to the subject when making pairwise assessments.

GROUP PROCESSES

In a group situation, members prepare the structure diagram, develop the factors and alternatives, and make the assessments necessary for making pairwise comparisons. While a certain amount of consensus is needed for the judgmental process, the task can be easily managed by a team leader. Personal computers can be used for the computations.

REFERENCES

Amsden, R.T., and Amsden, D.M., "A Look at QC Circles," *Quality Assurance: Methods, Management, and Motivation* (H.J. Bajaria, editor), Dearborn, Michigan: Society of Manufacturing Engineers, 1981, pp. 225-230.

Bajaria, H.J., "Methods of Quality Control," *Quality Assurance: Methods, Management, and Motivation* (H.J. Bajaria, editor). Dearborn, Michigan: Society of Manufacturing Engineers, 1981, pp. 53-58.

Bajaria, H.J. (editor), *Quality Assurance: Methods, Management and Motivation,* Dearborn, Michigan: Society of Manufacturing Engineers, 1981.

Beardsley, J.F., *Quality Circles,* Midwest City, Oklahoma: International Association of Quality Circles, 1982.

Beene, K.D., and Sheats, P., "Functional Roles of Group Members," *Journal of Social Issues* (1948), 4:41-49.

Bormann, E.G., *Discussion and Group Methods: Theory and Practice,* New York: Harper & Row, 1969.

Bradford, D.L., and Cohen, A.R., *Managing for Excellence,* New York: John Wiley and Sons, 1984.

Crosby, P.B., *Quality is Free,* New York: McGraw-Hill Book Company, 1979.

Davis, C.R., "A Strategy for Improving Product Quality Through Quality Awareness and Participative Management," *Quality Assurance: Methods, Management, and Motivation* (H.J. Bajaria, editor), Dearborn, Michigan: Society of Manufacturing Engineers, 1981, pp. 17-26.

Dewar, D.L., *The Quality Circle Guide to Participative Management*, Englewood Cliffs, New Jersey: Prentice-Hall Inc., 1980.

Drucker, P., *Managing in Turbulent Times*, London: Pan Books, 1980.

Fisher, B.A., *Small Group Decision Making: Communication and the Group Process*, New York: McGraw-Hill, Inc., 1974.

Freund, R.A., "The Role of Quality Technology," *Quality Assurance: Methods, Management, and Motivation* (H.J. Bajaria, editor), Dearborn, Michigan: Society of Manufacturing Engineers, 1981, pp. 10-13.

Glaser, R., and Glaser, C., *Managing by Design*, Reading, Massachusetts: Addison-Wesley Publishing Company, 1981.

Herzberg, F., *Work and the Nature of Man*, Cleveland, Ohio: The World Publishing Company, 1966.

Ingle, S., *Quality Circles Master Guide: Increasing Productivity with People Power*, Englewood Cliffs, New Jersey: Prentice-Hall, Inc., 1982.

International Conference on Quality Control Proceedings, Tokyo: Union of Japanese Scientists and Engineers, 1978.

Ishikawa, K., *Guide to Quality Control*, Tokyo: Asian Productivity Organization, 1976.

Ishikawa, K., *QC Circle Koryo: General Principles of the QC Circle*, Tokyo: Union of Japanese Scientists and Engineers (JUSE), 1980.

Johnson, D.W., and Johnson, F.P., *Joining Together: Group Theory and Group Skills*, Englewood Cliffs, New Jersey: Prentice-Hall, Inc., 1982.

Katzan, H., *Management Support Systems: A Pragmatic Approach*, New York: Van Nostrand Reinhold Company, 1984.

Luft, J., *Of Human Interaction*, Palo Alto, California: National Press Books, 1969.

McKenny, J.L., and Keen, P.G.W., "How Managers' Minds Work," Harvard Business Review, *On Human Relations*, New York: Harper & Row, 1979, pp. 30-47.

Mintberg, H., "Planning on the Left Side and Managing on

the Right," Harvard Business Review, *On Human Relations,* New York: Harper & Row, 1979, pp. 4-10.

Peters, T., and Austin, N., *A Passion for Excellence,* New York: Random House, 1985.

Puri, S.C., and J.R. McWhinnie, "Quality Management Through Quality Indicators: A New Approach," *Quality Assurance: Methods, Management, and Motivation* (H.J. Bajaria, editor), Dearborn, Michigan: Society of Manufacturing Engineers, 1981, pp. 34-40.

Saaty, T.L., *Decision Making for Leaders,* Belmont, California: Lifetime Learning Publications (a division of Wadsworth, Inc.), 1982.

Schein, E.H., *Process Consultation: Its Role in Organizational Development,* Reading, Massachusetts: Addison-Wesley Publishing Company, 1967.

Schonberger, R.J., *Japanese Manufacturing Techniques,* New York: The Free Press, 1982.

Steiner, G.A., *Strategic Planning: What Every Manager Must Know,* New York: The Free Press, 1979.

Thomas, E.F., "Shortcomings of Current Motivational Techniques," *Quality Assurance: Methods, Management, and Motivation* (H.J. Bajaria, editor), Dearborn, Michigan: Society of Manufacturing Engineers, 1981, pp. 87-96.

Tuckman, B.W., "Developmental Sequence in Small Groups," *Psychological Bulletin* (1965): 63(6), pp. 384-399.

Veen, B., "Integration of TQC and Motivation Programs," *Quality Assurance: Methods, Management, and Motivation* (H.J. Bajaria, editor), Dearborn, Michigan: Society of Manufacturing Engineers, 1981, pp. 97-101.

Wilensky, R., *Planning and Understanding: A Computational Approach to Human Reasoning,* Reading, Massachusetts: Addison-Wesley Publishing Company, 1983.

INDEX